COOKING AT A GLANCE

PASTA

BLOOMSBURY

This edition published in 1995 by
BLOOMSBURY PUBLISHING PLC
2 Soho Square
London WIV SPE

Conceived and produced by
WELDON OWEN INC.
814 Montgomery Street
San Francisco, CA 94133
Telephone (415) 291-0100
Fax (415) 291-8841

A member of the Weldon Owen
Group of Companies
SYDNEY • LONDON • SAN FRANCISCO

ISBN: 0 7475 1986 2

A CIP record for this book is available
from the British Library

©Copyright 1994 Weldon Owen Inc.

A WELDON OWEN PRODUCTION

Printed by Kyodo Printing Co.
(S'pore) Pte Ltd
Printed in Singapore

2

Cover Recipe:
Classic Tomato Sauce, page 18, with ravioli
Opposite Page:
Pasta & Prawns in Asparagus
Sauce, page 56

WELDON OWEN INC.

PRESIDENT JOHN OWEN

PUBLISHER WENDELY HARVEY

MANAGING EDITOR TORI RITCHIE

CONTRIBUTING EDITOR JANE HORN

AUSTRALIA/UK EDITOR JANET BUNNY

DESIGNER PATTY HILL

ASSISTANT DESIGNER ANGELA WILLIAMS

PRODUCTION STEPHANIE SHERMAN, MICK
BAGNATO, JAMES OBATA, AND TARJI MICKELSON

FOOD PHOTOGRAPHER CHRIS SHORTEN

STEPS PHOTOGRAPHER KEVIN CANDLAND

FOOD STYLISTS SUSAN MASSEY
AND VICKI ROBERTS-RUSSELL

PROP STYLIST LAURA FERGUSON

ASSISTANT FOOD STYLIST DANIEL BECKER

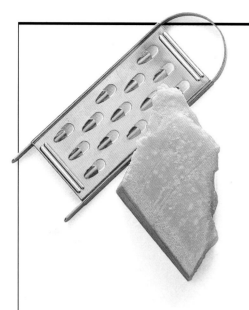

CONTENTS

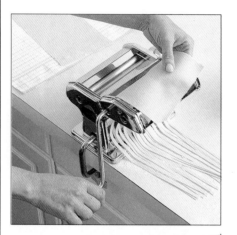

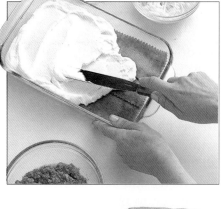

Introduction

PASTA: A SIMPLE ITALIAN WORD for a simple food that has appeared on Mediterranean and Asian tables for centuries. Yet pasta has become so popular with cooks everywhere in recent years that it has also come to mean a world of good eating in almost any language.

Why has pasta been elevated from ethnic favourite to international culinary superstar? Probably because it fits in so well with today's cooking style. People want food that is light, easily prepared, and superbly fresh, made with the season's best offerings. Pasta's subtle flavour and slightly chewy texture make it a perfect partner for fresh vegetables and herbs. And not only is pasta good to eat and quick to prepare, it also provides a healthy bonus: high-carbohydrate, low-fat pasta plays an important role in a well-balanced diet.

If long, thin spaghetti or tubular elbow macaroni are the pasta shapes that you are most familiar with, you are about to embark on a delicious voyage of discovery. The editors of *Cooking at a Glance* have created sixty new recipes that show off fresh and dried pasta in all its variety, including the wonderful packaged fresh pastas widely available in supermarkets today.

In the pages to come you will be introduced to little bow ties known as farfalle, to pleated radiatori, to circular ruote with spokes like wagon wheels, to tight little twists called fusilli, and to many more, including new and tempting interpretations of classics like tortellini, ravioli, and lasagne. You will also learn how easy it is to make plain, wholemeal, spinach, tomato, and herb pasta in your own kitchen.

An introductory chapter covers the basics of preparing homemade pasta and the best way to cook your own or purchased pasta so that it is served properly al dente. Next is a collection of sauces infused with aromatic fresh herbs, pungent garlic, and garden-picked vegetables that you will use again and again. Succeeding chapters explore the pleasures of particular types of pasta: ribbon, shaped, and stuffed pastas; layered pasta dishes; and hot and cold pasta salads. Every chapter is colour coded, and every recipe features a "steps-at-a-glance" box that uses these colours for quick reference to the photographic steps illustrating techniques used in the recipe. Tips appear throughout, from basic equipment needs to helpful hints to a glossary of ingredients. From first step to last, every recipe is guaranteed to please. Try elegant Stuffed Pasta Rolls the next time you entertain, or stir-fry a batch of Szechwan Chicken & Pasta for a quick after-work meal. Plan Sunday lunch around Spaghetti with Creamy Clam Sauce, an update of the popular seafood dish, or Baked Pasta & Cheddar with Ham, a sophisticated version of a childhood favourite. No matter which you choose, the result will be perfect, because it's all there for you, *at a glance.*

Stuffed Pasta Rolls, page 92

6

The Basics

Steps in Making Pasta

BASIC TOOLS FOR MAKING PASTA BY HAND

Making fresh pasta by hand requires mixing bowls and a wooden spoon plus a rolling pin to flatten the dough into paper-thin sheets and a knife to cut it into portions. To freeze the dough you will need a freezer-safe container.

ROLLING PIN

MIXING BOWLS

WOODEN SPOON

CHEF'S KNIFE

FREEZER-SAFE
CONTAINER

8

MAKING PASTA BY HAND

MAKING PASTA is a little like culinary alchemy. With a minimum of mixing, kneading, and shaping, the simplest of ingredients — flour, water, oil, salt, and eggs — are transformed into edible gold. Homemade pasta is easy to prepare, whether by hand or with a simple pasta machine available at most kitchenware shops.

Why make your own pasta if you can purchase it ready made? You can taste the difference. The result is more tender and delicate than packaged pasta, and will fully absorb whatever sauce coats it. However, good-quality purchased fresh or dried pasta can be almost as satisfying as the pasta you prepare from scratch.

On the pages to come you'll learn to make delicate narrow and wide ribbons, wrappers for stuffing manicotti and cannelloni, the little bundles known as ravioli and tortellini, and broad sheets for layered lasagne. You'll also discover the secrets of hand-shaping bow tie–shaped farfalle, the little cups called orecchiette, and more. For all of these and for any dish in the book that requires homemade pasta, use the basic recipe on page 14. The recipe is so simple that after the first few times you prepare it you probably won't even need to refer to it, but for now you might want to put a marker on that page for quick reference. Or, use purchased fresh pasta, available in the refrigerated case of many supermarkets or delicatessens.

This section demonstrates the essential steps in making pasta dough completely by hand. The remainder of the chapter describes how to mix pasta dough with a food processor, and the proper way to knead and roll the dough with a hand-cranked pasta maker that clamps onto a kitchen bench or table. Succeeding chapters detail how to cut and shape pasta dough and how to identify and use the myriad dry pasta shapes available. Even the best pasta, whether fresh or dried, can be ruined if improperly cooked. The steps on pages 12 and 13 explain this elementary but critical technique. Throughout this book, recipes require twice as much uncooked fresh pasta (homemade *or* purchased) as dried.

for herb pasta, add dried seasoning to flour mixture

for spinach pasta, add finely chopped cooked spinach to egg mixture

knead until dough is smooth and elastic (8 to 10 minutes)

STORING DOUGH

STEP 1 DIVIDING THE DOUGH

After kneading, shape the dough into a round; do not roll out. Divide the round into quarters or whatever portion size is specified in the recipe, using a sharp knife.

after cutting, shape each quarter portion into a ball and then flatten

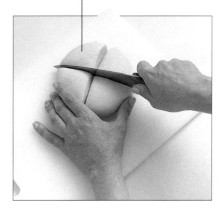

STEP 1 ADDING EGG MIXTURE TO FLOUR

Stir together flour and salt in a large mixing bowl. Make a well or depression in the centre. In another bowl combine eggs, water, and oil and pour liquid into the well of the flour mixture. Mix thoroughly with a wooden spoon.

STEP 2 KNEADING BY HAND

Turn out the dough onto a lightly floured work surface. To knead, curve your fingers over the edge of the dough and pull it toward you. Then push down and away with the heel of your hand. Give the dough a quarter turn, fold toward you, and repeat the process. Cover and let rest for 10 minutes before rolling out.

9

if the dough shrinks back while rolling, let it rest several minutes under a kitchen towel or sheet of plastic wrap, then continue

the surface of rolled-out dough must dry somewhat or it will stick together when cut

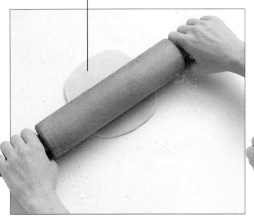

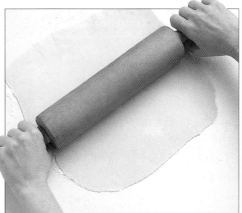

STEP 2 FREEZING DOUGH

Wrap each portion airtight in plastic wrap. Then store in a freezer-safe container or in heavy-duty freezer bags. The dough will keep in the freezer for up to 8 months.

to use, thaw several hours in the refrigerator or about 1 hour at room temperature

STEP 3 ROLLING THE DOUGH

Divide the dough into recipe-sized portions, usually in quarters. Set one portion on a floured work surface. Flatten with a rolling pin to about a ⅛ in/3 mm thickness. Cover the remaining dough with a kitchen towel or plastic wrap so it won't dry out, or freeze for later use as shown at right.

STEP 4 ROLLING DOUGH TO 1/16 IN/2 MM

Continue rolling the dough until it is 1/16 in/2 mm thick. A one-quarter portion will roll out to a square that is about 12x12 in/30x30 cm. After rolling, let the dough rest, uncovered, for 20 minutes so the surface will dry slightly.

Steps in Making Pasta

BASIC TOOLS FOR MAKING PASTA BY MACHINE

To prepare pasta by machine, use a small bowl, a measuring cup, a rubber spatula, and a food processor to mix the ingredients, and a hand-cranked pasta maker to knead and roll the dough.

FOOD PROCESSOR

PASTA MACHINE

LIQUID CUP MEASURE

SMALL BOWL

RUBBER SPATULA

10

MAKING PASTA BY MACHINE

W HEN PASTA DOUGH is mixed in a food processor, then rolled to paper thinness in a manual pasta maker, the whole process becomes almost effortless.

As usual, the food processor does its job quickly. Carefully watch the dough at every step. If you don't have a pasta machine, you can knead food processor dough with your hands and roll it out with a rolling pin as shown in steps 2, 3, and 4 on the previous page. However, the hand-turned pasta machine is inexpensive compared to most home appliances and small enough to store out of sight when not in use. If you make pasta often, it might be a sensible purchase because it takes most of the work out of kneading and rolling.

Start at the lowest setting, with the rollers wide apart; usually two passes through each setting will be enough. If the sheet of dough feeds through the rollers easily and looks smooth and silky, almost rubbery, without rough spots, turn to the next setting. If you have to crank hard, go back to a wider setting. Continue until the dough is the proper texture and thickness, usually 1/16 in/2 mm thick.

add chopped cooked spinach during this step if making spinach pasta by machine

STEP 1 PROCESSING DRY INGREDIENTS
Place flour, salt, and eggs in the work bowl of a food processor. Cover and process with a pulsing action until the mixture is the consistency of fine crumbs. This happens very quickly, so don't overprocess.

stir the liquid ingredients with a fork before pouring so they will blend more smoothly

if you let the dough rest after processing it will be easier to roll out

STEP 2 ADDING LIQUID

Put water, oil, and any other liquid in a measuring cup with a lip. With the processor running, slowly pour the liquid through the feed tube into the work bowl. The flour mixture will begin to form a cohesive mass.

STEP 3 FORMING A BALL

Continue processing the mixture only until the dough forms a ball. Stop once or twice to scrape down the sides of the work bowl so all the ingredients are incorporated into the dough. Remove from the work bowl, cover, and let rest 10 minutes.

11

sprinkle dough lightly with flour before each pass through the machine so it doesn't stick

when done, let dough sheet rest for 20 minutes on a lightly floured towel before shaping

if dough becomes too long to handle, cut it in half

STEP 4 KNEADING IN PASTA MACHINE

Divide the dough into 4 portions or as directed in the recipe. Cover unused dough or freeze (see page 9). Flatten one portion and feed through the rollers at the widest setting. Fold in half or thirds, give a quarter turn, and run through the same setting. Repeat until the dough is smooth and no longer tears.

STEP 5 ROLLING IN PASTA MACHINE

Turn to the next narrow setting. Lightly flour the dough, fold, give a quarter turn, and pass through the machine again. Repeat folding, turning, and rolling at increasingly higher (narrower) settings until the dough is 1/16 in/2 mm thick.

Steps in Making Pasta

BASIC TOOLS FOR COOKING PASTA

A large pasta pot lets pasta tumble freely in the bubbling water. The cooking liquid drains away afterwards through a strainer insert or free-standing colander. Use a pasta rake for tossing and serving long strands.

COLANDER

WOODEN PASTA RAKE

PASTA POT

PLASTIC PASTA RAKE

12

COOKING PASTA

ALWAYS USE a large pot so pasta can circulate freely in vigorously boiling water with room to expand as it cooks. If the pot is too small, the pasta will stick together; you also risk an overflow of the scalding, bubbling liquid. A pasta pot with a strainer insert is practical: It is the right size and lets you drain off the water with very little effort because the water flows back into the pot when you lift the insert. Salt may be added to the water for flavour and oil helps keep pasta from sticking, but neither is a must.

Fresh pasta never needs more than a few minutes to cook. Dried ribbons and shapes take longer; times vary from 8 to 15 minutes (check the package for recommended cooking times). Both types are done when the texture is tender but still slightly chewy and no traces of raw pasta remain when you bite into a piece — a quality described as "al dente." Drain, then transfer to a warm serving bowl and toss immediately with sauce or use as directed in the recipe. A pasta rake in wood, metal, or plastic works best for tossing and serving pasta strands.

for long strands, like spaghetti, dip one end of the batch in water until softened, then curl it around pan and lower it into the water

STEP 1 ADDING PASTA TO WATER

Fill a large pot with 3 qt/3 l of water (for 4 to 8 oz/125 to 250 g of pasta). Bring to a vigorous, rolling boil. Add 1 teaspoon of salt and 1 tablespoon of oil, if desired. Then add the pasta, a little at a time, so the water stays at the boil.

adjust the heat, if necessary, to keep the water boiling

STEP 2 STIRRING OCCASIONALLY

Stir occasionally with a wooden spoon or pasta rake to keep the strands or pieces from sticking together as they swirl around in the water.

For best flavour and texture, drain pasta thoroughly so no cooking water sticks to the pieces and dilutes the sauce.

the Italians say pasta is done when it is *al dente,* or "to the tooth"

STEP 3 TESTING FOR DONENESS

Near the end of cooking time, taste often to check for doneness. Pasta is ready when the texture is tender, but still slightly firm, or "al dente." Don't let the pasta sit in the cooking water or it will overcook and get mushy.

TIP BOX

TWO WAYS TO DRAIN

STEP 1 REMOVING DRAINER INSERT

If using a pasta pot with an insert, lift up the insert by the handles (protect your hands with oven pads, if necessary). The cooking water will drain back into the pot.

give the insert a few shakes to remove any remaining water from the pasta

STEP 2 DRAINING IN A COLANDER

Stand a colander in the sink. If using a standard pot without a drainer insert, pour the pasta and water into the colander as soon as the pasta is done.

13

Homemade Pasta

STEPS AT A GLANCE	Page
MAKING PASTA	8–11

Preparation Time: 1¼ hours

INGREDIENTS

8	OZ/250 G PLAIN FLOUR
1/2	TEASPOON SALT
2	BEATEN EGGS
3	FL OZ/80 ML WATER
1	TEASPOON OLIVE OIL *OR* COOKING OIL
1-1/2	OZ/45 G PLAIN FLOUR

*T*his simple dough can be used for every recipe in this book that requires fresh pasta. Although quick to prepare, to save more time you can make the dough ahead and freeze it (see the tip box on page 9 for freezing and thawing directions). To substitute fresh pasta in a recipe that specifies dried, use 8 oz/250 g fresh for every 4 oz/125 g of dried pasta.

■ In a large mixing bowl stir together the 8 oz/250 g flour and the salt. Make a well in the centre of the mixture.

■ In a small mixing bowl stir together the eggs, water, and olive oil or cooking oil. Add to the flour mixture and mix well.

■ Sprinkle kneading surface with the 1½ oz/45 g flour. (Spinach, wholemeal, and tomato variations may not require the addition of any or all of this flour.) Turn dough out onto floured surface. Knead till dough is smooth and elastic (8 to 10 minutes total). Cover and let rest for 10 minutes.

■ Divide dough into quarters. On a lightly floured surface, roll each quarter into a 12-in/30-cm square about 1/16 in/2 mm thick. Let stand for about 20 minutes, or till slightly dry. Or, if using a pasta machine, pass each quarter of dough through machine, according to manufacturer's directions, till 1/16 in/2 mm thick. Shape or stuff as desired, or as directed in recipe.

■ To dry ribbons, hang pasta from a pasta-drying rack or clothes hanger, or toss with flour, shape into loose bundles, and place on a floured baking sheet. Let dry overnight or till completely dry. Place in an airtight container and refrigerate for up to 3 days. Or, dry the pasta for at least 1 hour. Seal it in a freezer bag or container. Freeze for up to 8 months.

Makes four 4-oz/125-g portions pasta (1 lb/500 g total)

■ **For Herb Pasta,** prepare pasta as directed, *except* add 1 teaspoon *dried basil, marjoram, or sage,* crushed, to flour mixture.

■ **For Spinach Pasta,** prepare pasta as directed, *except* decrease the water to 3 tablespoons and add 2½ oz/75 g very finely chopped cooked *spinach,* well drained, to the egg mixture.

■ **For Wholemeal Pasta,** prepare pasta as directed, *except* substitute *wholemeal flour* for the plain flour.

■ **For Tomato Pasta,** prepare pasta as directed, *except* substitute *tomato paste* for the water.

Per portion plain pasta: 292 calories, 10 g protein, 51 g carbohydrate, 4 g total fat (1 g saturated), 107 mg cholesterol, 300 mg sodium, 102 mg potassium

14

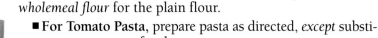
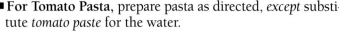
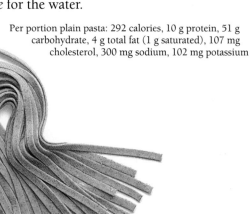

Basic Sauces

Steps in Preparing Sauce Ingredients

BASIC TOOLS FOR PREPARING SAUCE INGREDIENTS

Use knives and kitchen scissors to peel, slice, or chop vegetables and snip leafy herbs. Special tools include a press
for mincing garlic and a grater with fine holes for Parmesan.
A colander, bowl, and measuring cup hold ingredients.

COLANDER

SMALL BOWL

MEASURING CUP

CUTTING BOARD, PARMESAN GRATER, AND GARLIC PRESS

SCISSORS

CHEF'S KNIFE

SMALL, SHARP KNIFE

16

FAVOURITE SAUCES for pasta range from the simplicity of
garlic-infused olive oil or melted butter — for which
no recipe is needed — to herbal pestos and rich, complex
concoctions of cream, cheese, and eggs. Tomatoes and
pasta are a classic pairing with endless uses. In this chapter, you'll find a selection of basic sauces that can be
served over your favourite hot cooked pasta or used as
directed in other recipes in this book.

As with all dishes, a pasta sauce is only as good as
what you put into it. For red sauces, fully ripened fresh
plum (Roma) tomatoes are best. They are meaty and
juicy, not watery, and cook down into a thicker mixture.
If they aren't available, canned plum tomatoes (also some-
times labelled "Italian-style tomatoes") are preferable to
fresh ones that are unripe or flavourless. Fresh herbs,
whether basil, parsley, or oregano, should look lively, not
wilted, while dried herbs should be less than 6 months
old and have a characteristic aroma. Finally, there is no
comparison between Parmesan or other hard cheese,
hand-grated from a fresh wedge, and packaged grated
cheese. Resist the temptation to use pre-grated cheeses
and you'll find your sauces taste better than ever.

in the boiling water, the tomato skin will split at the X and peel away easily

STEP 1 PEELING TOMATOES

Cut an X in the blossom end of the tomato with the point
of a knife, then plunge the tomato into boiling water for
20 to 30 seconds to loosen the skin. Transfer to a colander to drain. When cool enough to handle, peel off the
skin by pulling it away with a small, sharp knife.

stubborn seeds can
also be coaxed out with
a knife or your finger

if the recipe calls for
drained tomatoes, pour
into a sieve, then cut up

to grate a large amount of
Parmesan cheese, drop chunks
into a running food processor
fitted with a metal blade

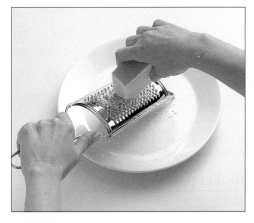

STEP 2 SEEDING TOMATOES

Cut the peeled tomato in half crosswise with a sharp knife. Hold the cut half upside down over the sink and squeeze gently to force out most of the seeds.

STEP 3 CUTTING UP TINNED TOMATOES

Insert a pair of sharp kitchen scissors with long blades into the can of whole tomatoes (no need to drain off the juice). Open and close the blades to cut the tomatoes into small pieces. Or, pour tomatoes into a bowl and then cut up.

STEP 4 GRATING FRESH PARMESAN

Rub a chunk of fresh Parmesan cheese across the holes of a hand grater. If you grate fresh cheese often, you may want to purchase a hand-turned winder-style grater that you can bring to the table.

17

you can also chop delicate herbs
with a knife, but snipping with
scissors is gentler and there is
less chance of mashing the leaves

you can also mince
garlic with a knife

grip the onion half
with your fingers to
keep it steady

STEP 5 CHOPPING FRESH HERBS

Strip the leaves of fresh herbs from their stems. Discard the stems and place the leaves in a measuring cup or bowl. Snip into small pieces with kitchen scissors.

STEP 6 MINCING GARLIC

Remove a clove of garlic from the head. Peel away the papery skin unless your garlic press will mince cloves with the skin intact. Squeeze the arms of the press together to force the garlic through the holes into a bowl.

STEP 7 CHOPPING ONIONS

Halve the onion lengthwise. Place one half, cut-side down, on a work surface. With a sharp knife, make a series of horizontal cuts almost to the root end and parallel to the work surface. Then make a series of evenly spaced vertical cuts from the top of the onion to the work surface. Finally, slice across the onion to create pieces.

Classic Tomato Sauce

Preparation Time: 40 minutes
Cooking Time: 25 minutes

INGREDIENTS

4	LB/2 KG RIPE PLUM (ROMA) TOMATOES *OR* 45 OZ/1.3 KG TINNED WHOLE ITALIAN-STYLE TOMATOES, WITH JUICE
2	TABLESPOONS OLIVE OIL *OR* COOKING OIL
2	CLOVES GARLIC, MINCED
1/2	TEASPOON SALT
1/2	TEASPOON SUGAR
1/4	TEASPOON PEPPER
1	OZ/30 G CHOPPED FRESH BASIL, OREGANO, *OR* PARSLEY

*I*f you like your tomato sauce chunky, skip the blending *or processing step and serve it hot from the pan. If you like, add meatballs to the sauce (see recipe, page 46).*

■ Peel, seed, and finely chop the fresh plum tomatoes, if using. In a large saucepan or Dutch oven, heat olive oil or cooking oil over medium heat. Add fresh or undrained tinned tomatoes, garlic, salt (omit if using tinned tomatoes), sugar, and pepper. Bring to boiling; reduce heat. Simmer, uncovered, for about 20 minutes, or to desired consistency. Place about half the sauce in a food processor bowl or blender container; process or blend till smooth. Return blended tomato mixture to saucepan. Stir in basil, oregano, or parsley. Cook for 5 minutes more.

Makes about 32 fl oz/1 litre

Per 8 fl oz/250 ml: 160 calories, 4 g protein, 22 g carbohydrate, 8 g total fat (1 g saturated), 0 mg cholesterol, 308 mg sodium, 1,030 mg potassium

STEPS IN MAKING TOMATO SAUCE

STEP 1 **SIMMERING SAUCE**

To achieve the desired consistency, bring the sauce ingredients to a boil, then reduce the heat and simmer uncovered, stirring now and then. This allows the excess liquid to evaporate and the flavours to become concentrated. When the tomatoes are broken down and the sauce is no longer runny, the sauce is done.

STEP 2 **BLENDING SAUCE**

Purée about half of the sauce in a blender or food processor. Return to the saucepan; add chopped herbs (fresh herbs are added at the last minute to preserve their fresh flavour). Cook 5 minutes more.

All pasta cooks should have a basic
tomato sauce in their repertoire and a
supply ready-made in the freezer to use
at a moment's notice.

The ancient city of Bologna, Italy, gave its name to
a tasty meat sauce that makes a hearty meal
when combined with any pasta shape.
Italians also call the sauce *ragù*.

Bolognese Sauce

Preparation Time: 30 minutes
Cooking Time: 38 to 40 minutes

INGREDIENTS

2	LB/1 KG RIPE PLUM (ROMA) TOMATOES *OR* 30 OZ/940 G TINNED WHOLE ITALIAN-STYLE TOMATOES, DRAINED
12	OZ/375 G LEAN MINCED BEEF
5	OZ/155 G FINELY CHOPPED ONION
2-1/2	OZ/75 G FINELY CHOPPED CARROT
2-1/2	OZ/75 G FINELY CHOPPED CELERY
2	SLICES BACON, FINELY CHOPPED
4	FL OZ/125 ML DRY RED WINE
6	FL OZ/180 ML HEAVY (DOUBLE) CREAM
1/2	TEASPOON SALT
1/4	TEASPOON PEPPER
1/8	TEASPOON GROUND NUTMEG

*E*xperiment with substituting Italian-style sausage or smoked sausage for the beef, or use a combination of veal and pork, which is the mark of a traditional Bolognese sauce.

■ Peel and seed fresh plum tomatoes, if using. In a food processor bowl or blender container process or blend fresh or tinned tomatoes till smooth; set aside.

■ In a large frying pan cook minced beef, onion, carrot, celery, and bacon for 5 minutes, or till meat is brown and vegetables are tender, stirring to break the meat into tiny pieces. Drain off fat. Add the wine. Bring to boiling; reduce heat. Simmer, uncovered, for 3 to 5 minutes, or till nearly all of the liquid has evaporated, stirring occasionally.

■ Stir in tomatoes. Cover and simmer for 30 minutes, or to desired consistency, stirring occasionally. Stir in cream, salt (omit if using tinned tomatoes), pepper, and nutmeg. Cook a few minutes more to heat through.

Makes 32 fl oz/1 litre

Per 8 fl oz/250 ml: 436 calories, 21 g protein, 22 g carbohydrate, 29 g total fat (15 g saturated), 117 mg cholesterol, 428 mg sodium, 1,069 mg potassium

21

STEPS IN MAKING BOLOGNESE SAUCE

STEP 1 **GRATING NUTMEG**
Rub a whole nutmeg across the grating holes of a nutmeg grater. Work over a piece of waxed paper or a bowl to collect the grated spice. Packaged ground nutmeg is an acceptable substitute for fresh, but it won't be as aromatic or flavoursome.

STEP 2 **BROWNING MEAT**
Cook the meat until it is brown and the vegetables are tender, stirring with a wooden spoon to break the minced meat into little pieces.

STEP 3 **ADDING CREAM**
Cream is added last to thicken and enrich the sauce. Pour it in while stirring to keep the cream from boiling over. Stir to blend thoroughly and cook a few minutes more to heat through.

Pesto

Preparation Time: 15 minutes

INGREDIENTS

1-1/2	OZ/45 G FIRMLY PACKED FRESH BASIL LEAVES
1	OZ/30 G GRATED PARMESAN CHEESE
1	OZ/30 G GRATED ROMANO CHEESE
1-1/2	OZ/45 G PINE NUTS *OR* FLAKED ALMONDS
1	LARGE CLOVE GARLIC, SLICED
1/8	TEASPOON SALT
2	FL OZ/60 ML OLIVE OIL *OR* COOKING OIL

A little pesto has a lot of flavour, so for a simple accompaniment for 2 to 3 people, use about 2 oz/60 ml of pesto tossed with 4 oz/125 g dried or 8 oz/250 g fresh pasta, cooked and drained.

■ In a food processor bowl or blender container combine basil, Parmesan cheese, Romano cheese, pine nuts or almonds, garlic, and salt. Pour in olive oil or cooking oil. Cover and process or blend with several on/off turns till a purée forms, stopping the machine several times and cleaning the sides with a rubber spatula. Store any remaining pesto in 2-fl oz/60-ml portions, wrapped and frozen for up to 1 year or refrigerated for up to 2 days. Before using, bring to room temperature.

Makes 6 fl oz/180 ml

Per tablespoon: 98 calories, 3 g protein, 1 g carbohydrate, 8 g total fat (2 g saturated), 4 mg cholesterol, 89 mg sodium, 74 mg potassium

STEPS IN MAKING PESTO

STEP 1 **ADDING INGREDIENTS**
Pour oil over the other pesto ingredients. The work bowl of the food processor should be fitted with the metal blade.

STEP 2 **FINISHING SAUCE**
Process with a few on/off pulses until a purée forms. Scrape down the sides of the work bowl a few times between pulses to blend.

STEP 3 **STORING SAUCE**
Spoon 2-fl oz/60-ml portions into small freezer or refrigerator containers. Before securing the lid, cover the pesto surface with plastic wrap to prevent browning. The sauce will keep, frozen, for up to 1 year.

Smooth, fragrant pesto coats strands
of pasta with the incomparable
flavour of fresh-picked basil.

Tomato-Vegetable Sauce

STEPS AT A GLANCE	Page
PREPARING SAUCE INGREDIENTS	16
SIMMERING SAUCE	18

Preparation Time: 20 minutes
Cooking Time: 20 to 25 minutes

INGREDIENTS

8	OZ/250 G FRESH MUSHROOMS, THINLY SLICED
2-1/2	OZ/75 G CHOPPED ONION
2	CLOVES GARLIC, MINCED
1	TABLESPOON OLIVE OIL *OR* COOKING OIL
10	OZ/315 G SHREDDED ZUCCHINI (COURGETTES)
15	OZ/470 G TINNED ITALIAN-STYLE CHUNKY TOMATO SAUCE
4	FL OZ/125 ML DRY RED WINE
1	TABLESPOON CHOPPED FRESH SAGE
1/4	TEASPOON SALT
1/4	TEASPOON PEPPER

This sauce is chunkier and more complex than a simple tomato sauce. Red wine adds body, and sliced mushrooms and shredded zucchini (courgettes) lend texture and depth of flavour.

*T*his traditional Italian sauce is never made with meat. Spoon it over hot cooked pasta and sprinkle with a little feta cheese or Parmesan cheese for a scrumptious vegetarian dish.

■ In a large frying pan cook mushrooms, onion, and garlic in hot olive oil or cooking oil for 5 minutes, stirring constantly. Add zucchini (courgettes) and cook for 5 minutes, or till vegetables are tender but not brown. Add tomato sauce, wine, sage, salt, and pepper. Bring to boiling; reduce heat. Simmer, uncovered, for 10 to 15 minutes, or to desired consistency, stirring frequently.
Makes 32 fl oz/1 litre

Per 8 fl oz/250 ml: 115 calories, 3 g protein, 15 g carbohydrate, 4 g total fat (1 g saturated), 0 mg cholesterol, 798 mg sodium, 785 mg potassium

Hearty Sausage & Tomato Sauce

*A*djust *the level of heat to your liking by selecting either plain or hot Italian sausage meat. Besides serving this sauce over pasta, you could also use it as a base for a hot and spicy chili sauce.*

■ Peel, seed, and chop the fresh plum tomatoes, if using.

■ In a large saucepan cook the Italian sausage, onion, green pepper, and garlic for 5 minutes, or till sausage is brown. Drain off fat. Carefully stir in the fresh or undrained tinned tomatoes, tomato paste, salt, oregano, basil, and red pepper. Bring to boiling; reduce heat. Cover and simmer for 30 minutes. Then uncover and simmer for 10 to 15 minutes more, or to desired consistency, stirring occasionally.

Makes 32 fl oz/1 litre

Per 8 fl oz/250 ml: 313 calories, 17 g protein, 25 g carbohydrate, 17 g total fat (6 g saturated), 49 mg cholesterol, 898 mg sodium, 1,274 mg potassium

INGREDIENTS

2	LB/1 KG RIPE PLUM (ROMA) TOMATOES OR 30 OZ/940 G TINNED ITALIAN-STYLE TOMATOES, CUT UP, DRAINED
12	OZ/375 G ITALIAN-STYLE SAUSAGE MEAT (CASINGS REMOVED)
2-1/2	OZ/75 G CHOPPED ONION
2	OZ/60 G FINELY CHOPPED GREEN PEPPER (CAPSICUM)
2	CLOVES GARLIC, MINCED
6	OZ/185 G TOMATO PASTE
1/2	TEASPOON SALT
1/2	TEASPOON DRIED OREGANO, CRUSHED
1/2	TEASPOON DRIED BASIL, CRUSHED
1/4	TEASPOON GROUND RED PEPPER (CAYENNE)

Preparation Time: 30 minutes
Cooking Time: 45 to 50 minutes

Combine this robust meat sauce with an equally substantial pasta such as penne.

Creamy Parmesan Sauce

Preparation Time: 50 minutes
Cooking Time: 2 to 10 minutes

INGREDIENTS

3	FL OZ/80 ML LIGHT (SINGLE) *OR* HEAVY (DOUBLE) CREAM
2	TABLESPOONS MARGARINE *OR* BUTTER
4	OZ/125 G DRIED *OR* 8 OZ/250 G FRESH TOMATO, HERB, *OR* PLAIN FETTUCCINE
1-1/2	OZ/45 G GRATED PARMESAN CHEESE
1/4	TEASPOON SALT
1	SMALL CLOVE GARLIC, MINCED
1	TABLESPOON CHOPPED FRESH BASIL *OR* FRESH PARSLEY (OPTIONAL)
	COARSELY GROUND BLACK PEPPER (OPTIONAL)

*C*ombine this rich cheese sauce with pasta ribbons and you have the classic pasta dish, *fettuccine Alfredo. As the sauce is poured over the cooked pasta, the heat cooks the sauce, causing the cream to thicken slightly and the cheese to melt.*

■ Allow cream and margarine or butter to come to room temperature (about 40 minutes).

■ In a large saucepan or pasta pot bring 3 qt/3 l water to boiling. Add pasta. Reduce heat slightly. Boil, uncovered, for 8 to 10 minutes for dried pasta or 1½ to 2 minutes for fresh pasta, or till al dente, stirring occasionally. (Or, cook according to package directions.) Immediately drain.

■ Return pasta to the warm pan. Add Parmesan cheese, cream, margarine or butter, salt, and garlic. Toss gently till pasta is well coated. Transfer to a warm serving dish. If desired, sprinkle with basil or parsley and pepper. Serve immediately.

Serves 4 as an accompaniment or 2 as a main course

Per serving: 282 calories, 10 g protein, 35 g carbohydrate, 11 g total fat (4 g saturated), 13 mg cholesterol, 363 mg sodium, 78 mg potassium

Fresh tomato pasta provides a subtle contrast to this rich and creamy cheese sauce. Serve with a favourite grilled chop and fresh vegetable.

26

Ribbon Pasta

Steps in Cutting Ribbon Pasta

BASIC TOOLS FOR MAKING RIBBON PASTA

Cut sheets of fresh pasta into ribbons with a small, sharp knife or with a pasta machine. To dry, drape the noodles over the rods of a pasta drying rack or arrange them in a shallow baking tin.

PASTA DRYING RACK

CUTTING BOARD AND SHALLOW BAKING TIN

PASTA MACHINE

SMALL, SHARP KNIFE

28

AMONG THE MOST VERSATILE of all pastas are the silky, flat ribbons cut from fresh dough. Called by a variety of names, depending on the width of the noodle, all ribbon pastas are superb with creamy sauces, pesto, and tomato-based sauces.

Homemade pasta ribbons with straight edges can be cut with a sharp knife or with the roller blades of a pasta machine (only a commercial machine will produce ribbons with ruffled edges). The cutting blades of a hand-turned pasta machine are preset to two prescribed sizes: ¼ in/6 mm wide for fettuccine or ¹⁄₁₆ in/2 mm wide for fine noodles — a similar size to spaghetti. When you cut the dough with a knife, the strips can be the traditional widths or any that appeal to you, including wide lasagne sheets (see page 76).

After you have made the dough and rolled it out (see pages 9 and 11), it must rest on a towel, uncovered, for about 20 minutes to allow the surface to dry slightly. This step keeps the pasta from sticking when it is rolled and sliced with a knife or when it is fed through the machine. If the sheets are very long, cut them into a manageable length.

The steps opposite show how to create ribbons by cutting a sheet of rolled dough with a knife or with a hand-turned pasta machine. After you have cut the ribbons by either method, the pasta can dry for up to 1 hour before it is cooked. You can drape it over the dowels of a special wooden pasta rack, or wrap it into little nests and place in a lightly floured shallow baking tin. If the pasta will not be used immediately, let it dry completely, preferably overnight. Once dried, place it in an airtight container and store in the refrigerator for up to 3 days. To freeze for up to 8 months, let the ribbons dry for 1 hour, then seal in a freezer bag or container.

Homemade pasta that has been fully dried can be used interchangeably with packaged dried pasta in the recipes in this book. If cooking homemade ribbons right away, follow the directions given for *fresh* pasta.

rolling the dough into a tube makes it easier to slice into uniform ribbons

STEP 1 ROLLING UP DOUGH

After the surface of the thin dough sheet has dried slightly, roll up the sheet loosely like a jam roll. Don't squeeze the roll or the dough might stick together.

if your knife is dull it will compress the roll rather than slice it cleanly

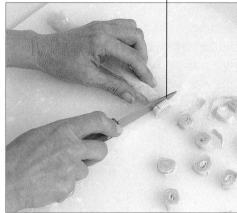

STEP 2 CUTTING DOUGH

Be sure your knife is very sharp. Slice the rolled dough into ¼-in/6-mm-wide strips for fettuccine, ⅛-in/3-mm-wide strips for linguine, or any width desired. For lasagne, cut the dough into 2½-in/6-cm-wide strips or wider sheets.

turn the handle clockwise only or the sheets won't pass through the blades

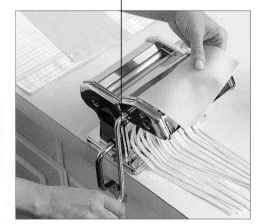

STEP 3 MACHINE-CUTTING FETTUCCINE

Secure the cutting attachment to the machine. If necessary, cut the rolled pasta sheet in half to match the width of the machine. Feed the pasta sheet through the ¼-in/6-mm-wide cutters.

to make ribbons of the same length, be sure the sheet is fed through evenly

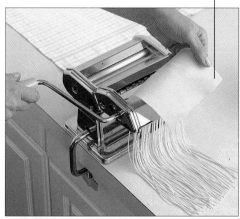

STEP 4 MACHINE-CUTTING FINE STRANDS

To make narrower strands, simply feed the rolled pasta sheet through the fine cutters, rather than the wider fettuccine blades. The fine strands will be more delicate than fettuccine, so handle them carefully. Use as you would spaghetti.

TIP BOX

DRYING PASTA

STEP 1 RACK DRYING

Loosely gather the ribbons and hang them on the dowels of a pasta-drying rack. One pound/half a kilo of ribbons should fit on most standard racks.

separate the strands so they won't stick together

STEP 2 DRYING ON A BAKING SHEET

Toss the pasta ribbons in flour and loosely shape into bundles. Arrange in a flour-dusted baking pan to dry.

use a metal baking pan or a jam-roll pan

29

Dried Pasta Ribbons and Strands

I N THE COMPLICATED HIERARCHY of Italian ribbon-pasta nomenclature, almost infinitesimal differences in width result in a different pasta. Names can also differ from one part of Italy to the other (for example,¼-in/6-mm-wide ribbons are called fettuccine in most regions, except in parts of the north where they are called tagliatelle), or from manufacturer to manufacturer. If a recipe requires a particular ribbon and you can't find it in the shop, be assured that you will come across another that is very similar to the one you need and that will work just as well. The best dried pasta is made from semolina flour or durum flour, both ground from hard durum wheat. Unlike fresh ribbon pasta, dried ribbon pasta may take the form of long, narrow rods (spaghetti and vermicelli), twisted strands (fusilli), or ruffled ribbons (mafalde).

Ribbon pastas also appear throughout Asia. While dried Italian pasta is made with flour, water, and some-times egg, Asian noodles use wheat, buckwheat, and rice flours, or vegetable starches made from beans or potatoes. Some incorporate egg, while others don't. Packaged Asian pastas are available at Asian groceries and some supermarkets.

30

you may want to reserve some sauce to pass at the table

STEP 1   TOSSING PASTA

Use a large bowl to allow plenty of room for tossing. Warm the bowl first to keep the pasta hot. Add about half of the sauce; toss to coat the strands, then add the remaining sauce and toss again.

Here's a look at some of the most widely available dried pasta ribbons and strands. Although similar, each is different enough to add its own unique character to a dish. Buckwheat noodles (soba) are used in Asian dishes.

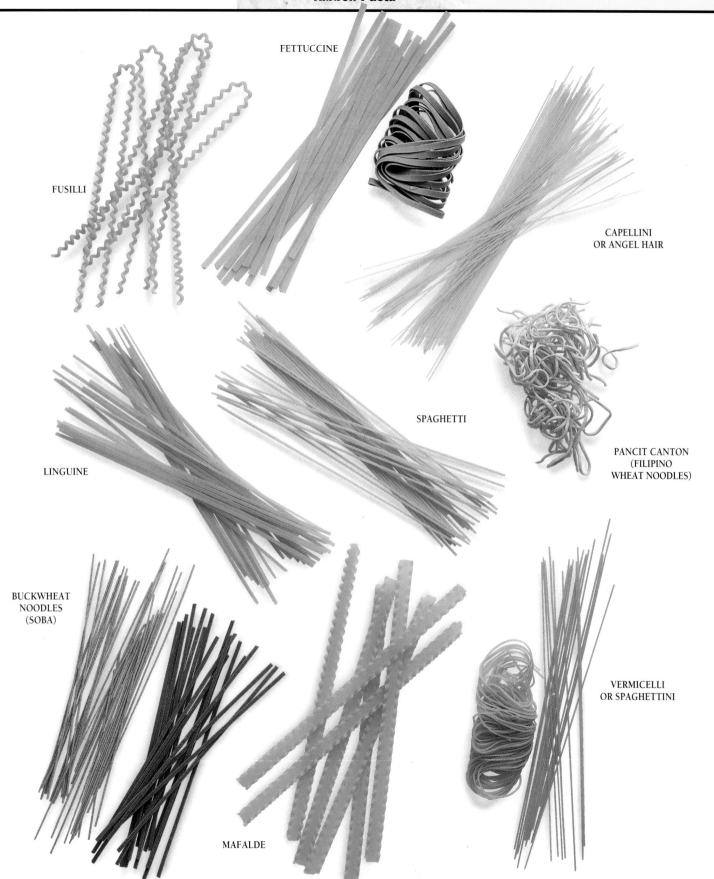

FUSILLI

FETTUCCINE

CAPELLINI
OR ANGEL HAIR

LINGUINE

SPAGHETTI

PANCIT CANTON
(FILIPINO
WHEAT NOODLES)

BUCKWHEAT
NOODLES
(SOBA)

VERMICELLI
OR SPAGHETTINI

MAFALDE

Fettuccine with Sweet & Sour Vegetables

Preparation Time: 20 minutes
Cooking Time: 28 to 30 minutes

INGREDIENTS

6	OZ/180 G KALE, SPINACH, *OR* SWISS CHARD (SILVERBEET)
6	OZ/180 G YELLOW BABY SQUASH *OR* COURGETTES, CUT INTO 1/4-IN/6-MM-THICK SLICES
4	OZ/125 G DRIED FETTUCCINE *OR* LINGUINE *OR* 8 OZ/250 G FRESH FETTUCCINE *OR* LINGUINE
1	OZ/30 G PANCETTA *OR* THICK-SLICED BACON, FINELY CHOPPED
2	TABLESPOONS OLIVE OIL *OR* COOKING OIL
2	OZ/60 G CHOPPED ONION
1	TABLESPOON PLAIN FLOUR
1	TABLESPOON SUGAR
1/2	TEASPOON SALT
1/8	TEASPOON PEPPER
6	FL OZ/180 ML CHICKEN STOCK
2	FL OZ/60 ML RED WINE VINEGAR

*I*f you decide to use spinach or Swiss chard (silverbeet) instead of kale, take note that they cook in much less time. Start by cooking the pasta, then cook the vegetables.

■ Wash the greens. Remove centre ribs, if necessary, and tear each leaf into bite-size pieces. In a large saucepan bring 8 fl oz/250 ml water to boiling. Add the kale and simmer, covered, for 25 minutes. Add baby squash or courgettes and spinach or Swiss chard (silverbeet), if using, and cook for 3 to 5 minutes, or till tender. Drain and keep warm.

■ Meanwhile, in a large saucepan or pasta pot bring 3 qt/3 l water to boiling. Add pasta. Reduce heat slightly. Boil, uncovered, for 8 to 10 minutes for dried pasta or 1½ to 2 minutes for fresh pasta, or till al dente, stirring occasionally. (Or, cook according to package directions.) Drain immediately.

■ Meanwhile, in a large frying pan cook the pancetta in hot oil. (If using bacon, cook it without the oil.) Add onion to cooked pancetta or bacon and cook till tender. Stir in flour, sugar, salt, and pepper. Stir in chicken stock and vinegar all at once. Cook and stir till thickened and bubbly. Cook and stir for 2 minutes more. Stir in cooked greens and squash; mix well. Spoon mixture over hot cooked pasta. Serve immediately.

Serves 4 as an accompaniment or entrée

Per serving: 255 calories, 8 g protein, 31 g carbohydrate, 11 g total fat (4 g saturated), 12 mg cholesterol, 535 mg sodium, 249 mg potassium

32

STEPS IN PREPARING MEAT AND VEGETABLES

STEP 1 **PREPARING GREENS**
Cut along either side of the centre rib of kale from top to bottom; discard the ribs and chop the leaves.

STEP 2 **DICING PANCETTA**
Make parallel cuts in one flat slice of pancetta. Turn the knife and slice across the cuts to form diced pieces.

STEP 3 **COOKING PANCETTA**
Heat the oil, then add the diced pancetta. Cook until browned and crisp on the edges, tossing to keep the pieces from sticking.

Pancetta (Italian bacon) seasons this tangy sauce brightened with greens and baby squash or courgettes.

Strands of pasta twine around a
colourful mixture of vegetables,
all coated with a creamy sauce.

34

Springtime Carbonara

Preparation Time: 20 minutes
Cooking Time: 18 to 19 minutes

INGREDIENTS

4	OZ/125 G BABY CARROTS
5	OZ/155 G FROZEN PEAS *OR* SHELLED FRESH PEAS
4	OZ/125 G FRESH ASPARAGUS, TRIMMED AND CUT INTO 2-IN/ 5-CM PIECES
6	OZ/185 G DRIED SPAGHETTI *OR* FETTUCCINE *OR* 12 OZ/375 G FRESH FETTUCCINE *OR* OTHER RIBBON PASTA
1	BEATEN EGG
8	FL OZ/250 ML LIGHT (SINGLE) CREAM
2	TABLESPOONS MARGARINE *OR* BUTTER
2	OZ/60 G GRATED PARMESAN CHEESE
2	TABLESPOONS CHOPPED FRESH CHIVES *OR* SPRING ONIONS
	PEPPER

*W*e call this "springtime" because vegetables replace the bacon used in traditional carbonara. However, with fresh vegetables available all year round, you can enjoy this delicious carbonara during the winter, too.

■ In a medium saucepan cook carrots in a small amount of boiling water for 10 minutes. Add peas and asparagus. Cook for 5 minutes more, or till vegetables are crisp-tender. Drain.

■ Meanwhile, in a large saucepan or pasta pot bring 3 qt/3 l water to boiling. Add pasta. Reduce heat slightly. Boil, uncovered, 8 to 12 minutes for dried pasta or 1½ to 2 minutes for fresh, or till al dente, stirring occasionally. (Or, cook according to package directions.) Return pasta to warm pan; add cooked vegetables.

■ In a medium saucepan combine the egg, cream, and margarine or butter. Cook and stir over medium heat till mixture just coats a metal spoon (about 3 to 4 minutes). Remove from heat. Immediately stir in the Parmesan cheese and chives or spring onions. Pour egg mixture over hot pasta and vegetables and toss to coat pasta. Transfer to a warm serving dish. Sprinkle with pepper. Serve immediately.

Serves 6 as an accompaniment or entrée

Per serving: 276 calories, 11 g protein, 31 g carbohydrate, 12 g total fat (7 g saturated), 65 mg cholesterol, 229 mg sodium, 257 mg potassium

STEPS IN MAKING CARBONARA SAUCE

STEP 1 TESTING EGG MIXTURE

Dip a spoon into the cooked egg mixture. The excess should drip off, leaving a creamy coating slightly thicker than milk. The coating should hold its shape when you wipe a finger across the back of the spoon.

STEP 2 CHOPPING CHIVES

Hold a bunch of chives with one hand (remove any damaged pieces). With kitchen scissors, snip off little tubes (about ¼ in/6 mm long) into a small bowl.

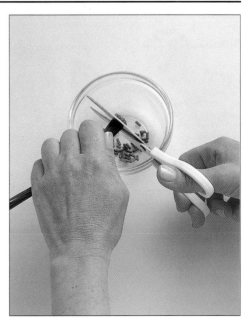

Pasta & Prawn Diavolo

Preparation Time: 25 minutes
Cooking Time: 8 to 12 minutes

INGREDIENTS

8	OZ/250 G DRIED SPAGHETTI, LINGUINE, *OR* FETTUCCINE *OR* 1 LB/500 G FRESH FETTUCCINE *OR* LINGUINE
4	OZ/125 G BROCCOLI FLORETS
8	FL OZ/250 ML CHICKEN STOCK
2	TABLESPOONS CORNFLOUR
2	TABLESPOONS DIJON-STYLE MUSTARD
2	TABLESPOONS LEMON JUICE
1	TABLESPOON DRAINED CAPERS
1	LB/500 G FRESH PRAWNS, PEELED AND DEVEINED, *OR* 12 OZ/375 G FROZEN PEELED AND DEVEINED PRAWNS, THAWED
2	TABLESPOONS OLIVE OIL *OR* COOKING OIL
1/2	TEASPOON HOT CHILI OIL *OR* 1/8 TEASPOON CHILI POWDER
	LEMON WEDGES (OPTIONAL)

*Y*ou can easily adjust the spiciness of this dish by increasing or decreasing the amount of chili you use, or by adding crushed red pepper flakes for a real kick.

■ In a large saucepan or pasta pot bring 3 qt/3 l water to boiling. Add pasta. Reduce heat slightly. Boil, uncovered, 8 to 12 minutes for dried pasta or 1½ to 2 minutes for fresh, or till al dente, stirring occasionally. (Or, cook according to package directions.) Add the broccoli to the boiling dried pasta during the last 5 minutes of cooking time. Drain immediately. (If using fresh pasta, cook the broccoli separately in a small amount of boiling water for about 5 minutes, or until crisp-tender. Drain and add to cooked pasta.)

■ Meanwhile, in a small mixing bowl stir together chicken stock, cornflour, mustard, lemon juice, and capers; set aside. In a large frying pan cook and stir prawns in hot olive oil or cooking oil and chili oil or powder over medium-high heat for 1 minute. Stir stock mixture; carefully add to pan. Cook and stir till thickened and bubbly. Cook and stir for 2 minutes more, or till prawns turn pink. Toss with pasta-broccoli mixture. If desired, garnish with lemon wedges.

Serves 4 as a main course

Per serving: 407 calories, 25 g protein, 51 g carbohydrate, 11 g total fat (2 g saturated), 131 mg cholesterol, 588 mg sodium, 408 mg potassium

STEPS IN MAKING PRAWN DIAVOLO

STEP 1 CUTTING FLORETS

Florets are the tightly closed heads that top each thick stalk of broccoli. Trim off the stalks and use them in another recipe. Halve or quarter the florets if large.

STEP 2 PEELING PRAWNS

With kitchen scissors or a paring knife, cut the shell along the curve of the back from head to tail end. The shell and legs should peel off in one piece. To devein, pull out and discard the dark vein that runs along the back.

STEP 3 COOKING PRAWNS

Add the stock mixture to the partially cooked prawns in the frying pan. Cook and stir an additional 2 minutes, or until the prawns turn pink and opaque.

Diavolo is synonymous with "spicy." In this quick-to-assemble seafood dish, mustard and chili oil provide the heat.

Tarragon and pungent blue-veined
Gorgonzola add punch to this creamy
sauce. A garnish of chopped toasted
pecans provides a crunchy contrast.

38

Fettuccine with Gorgonzola-Tarragon Sauce

*T*his pasta dish is rich with cream and the intense flavour of Gorgonzola. Offer some extra crumbled Gorgonzola with the pasta for the cheese-lovers at the table.

■ In a large saucepan or pasta pot bring 3 qt/3 l water to boiling. Add pasta. Reduce heat slightly. Boil, uncovered, 8 to 10 minutes for dried pasta or 1½ to 2 minutes for fresh, or till al dente, stirring occasionally. (Or, cook according to package directions.) Drain immediately. Return pasta to warm pan.

■ Meanwhile, in a small saucepan melt margarine or butter. Add the Gorgonzola cheese, cream, tarragon, and pepper. Cook and stir over medium heat till cheese is melted and mixture is smooth and heated through. Stir in Parmesan cheese. Pour sauce over pasta. Gently toss till pasta is coated. Transfer to a warm serving dish. Sprinkle with nuts. Serve immediately with extra cheese if desired.

Serves 4 as an accompaniment or entrée

Per serving: 253 calories, 10 g protein, 23 g carbohydrate, 13 g total fat (7 g saturated), 29 mg cholesterol, 377 mg sodium, 130 mg potassium

Preparation Time: 15 minutes
Cooking Time: 8 to 10 minutes

INGREDIENTS

4	OZ/125 G DRIED *OR* 8 OZ/250 G FRESH SPINACH FETTUCCINE *OR* LINGUINE
1	TABLESPOON MARGARINE *OR* BUTTER
2	OZ/60 G CRUMBLED GORGONZOLA CHEESE
2	FL OZ/60 ML LIGHT (SINGLE) CREAM
2	TABLESPOONS CHOPPED FRESH TARRAGON *OR* 1-1/2 TEASPOONS DRIED TARRAGON, CRUSHED
	DASH GROUND WHITE PEPPER *OR* BLACK PEPPER
1	OZ/30 G GRATED PARMESAN CHEESE
2	TABLESPOONS CHOPPED TOASTED PECANS *OR* WALNUTS

39

STEPS IN CRUMBLING CHEESE AND TOASTING NUTS

STEP 1 CRUMBLING GORGONZOLA

In order for the cheese to melt quickly and smoothly, it should be crumbled first. Put a chunk of cheese in a pie plate or on a dish. Crumble by breaking it up with a fork.

STEP 2 TOASTING NUTS

Spread the nuts in a metal pie plate. Bake in a preheated 350°F/180°C oven for 5 to 10 minutes, or until lightly browned. Stir once or twice so the nuts brown evenly.

Aglio e Olio with Fresh Sage

STEPS AT A GLANCE	Page
MAKING PASTA	8–14
CUTTING RIBBON PASTA	28

Preparation Time: 10 minutes
Cooking Time: 10 to 12 minutes

INGREDIENTS

4	OZ/125 G MAFALDE, SPAGHETTI, *OR* OTHER DRIED RIBBON PASTA *OR* 8 OZ/250 G FRESH FETTUCCINE
2	TABLESPOONS OLIVE OIL *OR* COOKING OIL
2	CLOVES GARLIC, MINCED
1	TABLESPOON CHOPPED FRESH SAGE *OR* 1/2 TEASPOON DRIED SAGE, CRUSHED
	SALT AND PEPPER
	GRATED PARMESAN CHEESE (OPTIONAL)

40

Ruffled ribbon pasta in a garlicky sauce flecked with bits of sage is the perfect accompaniment to roasted or grilled chicken.

*G*arlic (aglio) and oil (olio) are a classic Italian *combination. When sage is added, you have a light and delicious pasta sauce that can be made in a moment.*

■ In a large saucepan or pasta pot bring 3 qt/3 l water to boiling. Add pasta. Reduce heat slightly. Boil, uncovered, for 10 to 12 minutes for dried pasta or 1½ to 2 minutes for fresh, or till al dente, stirring occasionally. (Or, cook according to package directions.) Drain immediately. Return pasta to warm pan.

■ Meanwhile, in a small saucepan heat oil over medium heat. Add garlic and sage and cook and stir for 1 minute.

■ Toss sage mixture with hot pasta. Season to taste with salt and pepper. If desired, sprinkle with Parmesan cheese. Serve immediately.

Serves 4 as an accompaniment or entrée

Per serving: 175 calories, 4 g protein, 23 g carbohydrate, 7 g total fat (1 g saturated), 0 mg cholesterol, 35 mg sodium, 32 mg potassium

Straw & Hay with Wild Mushrooms in Cream

*P*our a little of the boiling water from the pasta pot into your serving bowl to heat it up quickly. Empty the water just before you are ready to fill the bowl with pasta.

■ In a large saucepan or pasta pot bring 3 qt/3 l water to boiling. Add pasta. Reduce heat slightly. Boil, uncovered, for 8 to 10 minutes for dried pasta or 1½ to 2 minutes for fresh, or till al dente, stirring occasionally. (Or, cook according to package directions.) Drain immediately. Return pasta to warm pan.

■ Meanwhile, in a large frying pan cook and stir spring onions and red or green pepper in hot margarine or butter over medium-high heat for 2 minutes. Add mushrooms; cook and stir for 2 minutes more, or till vegetables are tender. Stir in cream and heat through, but do not boil.

■ Pour mushroom-cream mixture over pasta and toss to coat pasta. Add Parmesan cheese and toss. Transfer to a warm serving dish. Sprinkle with pepper. Serve immediately.

Serves 6 as an accompaniment or entrée

Per serving: 277 calories, 9 g protein, 33 g carbohydrate, 12 g total fat (5 g saturated), 18 mg cholesterol, 170 mg sodium, 225 mg potassium

INGREDIENTS

4	OZ/125 G DRIED *OR* 8 OZ/250 G FRESH PLAIN FETTUCCINE
4	OZ/125 G DRIED *OR* 8 OZ/250 G FRESH SPINACH FETTUCCINE
1	OZ/30 G SLICED SPRING ONIONS
4	OZ/125 G FINELY CHOPPED RED *OR* GREEN PEPPER (CAPSICUM)
3	TABLESPOONS MARGARINE *OR* BUTTER
6	OZ/185 G FRESH SHIITAKE MUSHROOMS, SLICED
8	FL OZ/250 ML LIGHT (SINGLE) *OR* HEAVY (DOUBLE) CREAM
1	OZ/30 G GRATED PARMESAN CHEESE
	PEPPER

Preparation Time: 15 minutes
Cooking Time: 8 to 10 minutes

STEPS AT A GLANCE	Page
MAKING PASTA	8–14
CUTTING RIBBON PASTA	28
PREPARING SAUCE INGREDIENTS	16

41

The Italians call this contrasting mixture of yellow and green pasta "straw and hay."

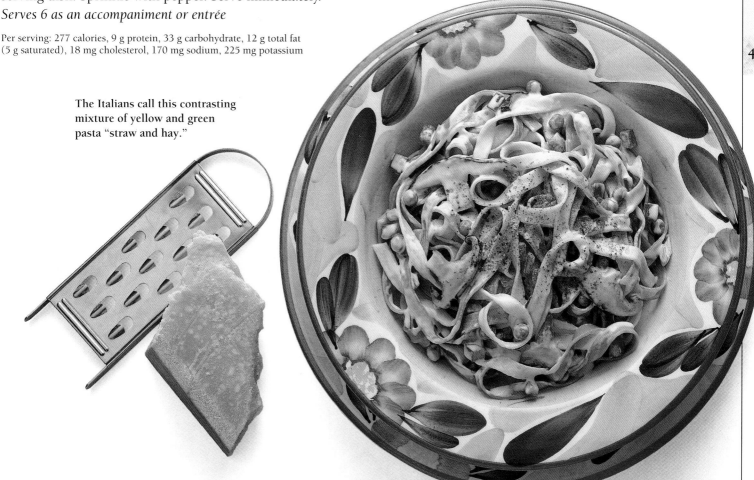

Spaghetti with Creamy Clam Sauce

Preparation Time: 20 minutes
Cooking Time: 8 to 12 minutes

INGREDIENTS

8	OZ/250 G DRIED SPAGHETTI OR LINGUINE OR 1 LB/500 G FRESH LINGUINE OR OTHER RIBBON PASTA

SAUCE

14	OZ/440 G TINNED MINCED CLAMS OR CHOPPED COOKED CLAMS
	LIGHT (SINGLE) CREAM OR MILK
2	OZ/60 G CHOPPED ONION
2	CLOVES GARLIC, MINCED
2	TABLESPOONS MARGARINE OR BUTTER
1	OZ/30 G PLAIN FLOUR
1/2	TEASPOON DRIED BASIL OR OREGANO, CRUSHED
1/4	TEASPOON SALT
1/4	TEASPOON PEPPER
2	TABLESPOONS CHOPPED FRESH PARSLEY
2	FL OZ/60 ML DRY WHITE WINE
1	OZ/30 G GRATED PARMESAN CHEESE

Sprinkle this seafood sauce with Parmesan cheese just before serving. It's always a good idea to grate a little extra to offer at the table.

*T*his creamy version of the ever-popular pasta with clam sauce cooks in minutes. If small tins of minced clams are pantry staples, you can prepare an enticing meal with very little notice. Serve with a green salad and crusty bread to soak up the sauce.

■ In a large saucepan or pasta pot bring 3 qt/3 l water to boiling. Add pasta. Reduce heat slightly. Boil, uncovered, for 8 to 12 minutes for dried pasta or 1½ to 2 minutes for fresh, or till al dente, stirring occasionally. (Or, cook according to package directions.) Drain immediately.

■ Meanwhile, drain clams, reserving liquid. Add enough light cream or milk to the liquid to make 14 fl oz/440 ml.(If using cooked clams, use 14 fl oz/440 ml light cream or milk.)

■ For sauce, in a medium saucepan cook the onion and garlic in hot margarine or butter for about 5 minutes, or till onion is tender but not brown. Stir in the flour, basil or oregano, salt, and pepper. Add the cream mixture all at once. Cook and stir till thickened and bubbly. Cook and stir for 1 minute more. Stir in the parsley, wine, and clams. Heat through.

■ Serve sauce over hot pasta. Sprinkle with Parmesan cheese. Serve immediately.

Serves 4 as a main course

Per serving: 551 calories, 21 g protein, 59 g carbohydrate, 25 g total fat (12 g saturated), 115 mg cholesterol, 401 mg sodium, 367 mg potassium

Turkey Tetrazzini

Preparation Time: 25 minutes
Baking Time: 20 minutes

Use leftover cooked turkey or chicken for a pasta dish with all the flavours of an elegant pie.

INGREDIENTS

6	OZ/185 G DRIED SPAGHETTI, VERMICELLI, *OR* CAPELLINI *OR* 12 OZ/375 G FRESH LINGUINE *OR* OTHER RIBBON PASTA
1	OZ/30 G DRIED TOMATOES (NOT OIL-PACKED) (8 HALVES)
5	OZ/155 G STEMMED AND SLICED FRESH SHIITAKE MUSHROOMS *OR* REGULAR MUSHROOMS
3	TABLESPOONS MARGARINE *OR* BUTTER
1	OZ/30 G PLAIN FLOUR
1/8	TEASPOON GROUND NUTMEG
12	FL OZ/375 ML LIGHT (SINGLE) CREAM *OR* MILK
8	FL OZ/250 ML CHICKEN STOCK
15	OZ/470 G CHOPPED COOKED TURKEY *OR* CHICKEN
2	TABLESPOONS DRY SHERRY
1	OZ/30 G GRATED PARMESAN CHEESE
1	OZ/30 G FLAKED ALMONDS

43

*A*ccording to most accounts, the opera singer Luisa Tetrazzini inspired the original version of this poultry-based dish almost a century ago.

■ In a large saucepan or pasta pot bring 3 qt/3 l water to boiling. Add pasta. Reduce heat slightly. Boil, uncovered, 10 to 12 minutes for spaghetti and 5 to 7 minutes for vermicelli or capellini, or 1½ to 2 minutes for fresh pasta, or till al dente, stirring occasionally. (Or, cook according to package directions.) Drain immediately.

■ Place dried tomatoes in a small bowl. Add enough hot water to cover; soak for 10 to 15 minutes, or till softened. Drain and pat dry. Chop tomatoes; set aside.

■ Meanwhile, in a large saucepan cook mushrooms in melted margarine or butter till tender. Stir in flour and nutmeg. Add light cream or milk and chicken stock all at once. Cook and stir till thickened and bubbly. Stir in turkey or chicken, sherry, and chopped tomatoes. Add cooked pasta; toss to coat.

■ Transfer to a 2-qt/2-l rectangular baking dish. Sprinkle with Parmesan cheese and almonds. Bake in a preheated 350°F/180°C oven for 20 minutes, or till heated through. Serve immediately.

Serves 6 as a main course

Per serving: 462 calories, 29 g protein, 37 g carbohydrate, 22 g total fat (7 g saturated), 79 mg cholesterol, 481 mg sodium, 576 mg potassium

STEPS AT A GLANCE	**Page**
COOKING PASTA	12

Pasta with Turkey & Tomatoes in Cream

Smoked turkey adds a subtle flavour to an elegant pasta sauce featuring both fresh and dried tomatoes.

Preparation Time: 20 minutes
Cooking Time: 20 minutes

INGREDIENTS

2	LB/1 KG RIPE PLUM (ROMA) TOMATOES *OR* 30 OZ/940 G TINNED ITALIAN-STYLE TOMATOES, CUT UP, WITH JUICE
2	CLOVES GARLIC, MINCED
1/2	TEASPOON SUGAR
1/4	TEASPOON SALT
1/8	TEASPOON PEPPER
4	FL OZ/125 ML HEAVY (DOUBLE) CREAM
12	OZ/375 G FULLY COOKED SMOKED TURKEY BREAST, CUT INTO 2X1/4-IN/5-CMX6-MM STRIPS
2	OZ/60 G DRAINED OIL-PACKED DRIED TOMATOES, CHOPPED
2	TABLESPOONS CHOPPED FRESH PARSLEY
8	OZ/250 G FUSILLI, LINGUINE, *OR* OTHER DRIED RIBBON PASTA *OR* 1 LB/500 G FRESH LINGUINE *OR* FETTUCCINE
1	OZ/30 G GRATED PARMESAN CHEESE (OPTIONAL)

*G*rind fresh black pepper over the top of this savoury pasta to give it a boost in flavour and in appearance. Garnish with Italian parsley.

■ Peel and chop fresh plum tomatoes, if using. In a large frying pan heat oil over medium heat. Add fresh or undrained tinned tomatoes, garlic, sugar, salt, and pepper. Bring to boiling; reduce heat. Boil gently, uncovered, for 15 minutes or till thickened, stirring occasionally. Gradually add the cream to the tomato mixture, stirring constantly. Add the turkey and dried tomatoes; heat through. Remove from heat; stir in parsley.

■ Meanwhile, in a large saucepan or pasta pot bring 3 qt/3 l water to boiling. Add pasta. Reduce heat slightly. Boil, uncovered, 15 minutes for dried fusilli and 8 to 10 minutes for dried linguine, or 1½ to 2 minutes for fresh pasta, or till al dente, stirring occasionally. (Or, cook according to package directions.) Drain immediately.

■ Serve sauce over pasta. If desired, sprinkle with Parmesan cheese. Serve immediately.

Serves 4 as a main course

Per serving: 493 calories, 29 g protein, 63 g carbohydrate, 15 g total fat (8 g saturated), 77 mg cholesterol, 1,045 mg sodium, 1,076 mg potassium

44

Toasted Vermicelli with Fresh Salsa

*T*o give the sauce even more of a Spanish flavour, use 8 fl oz/250 ml of clam juice and 8 fl oz/250 ml of chicken stock, instead of 16 fl oz/500 ml of chicken stock. This makes a tasty complement for grilled fish.

■ In a large frying pan cook pasta, onion, and garlic in hot oil for 5 minutes, or till pasta is golden and onion is tender, stirring constantly. Gently stir in 2 tomatoes, the chicken stock, chilies, oregano, cumin, and salt. Bring to boiling; reduce heat. Simmer, uncovered, for about 8 minutes, or till pasta is al dente. Stir in coriander. Transfer to a serving dish. If desired, garnish with chopped tomatoes.

Serves 6 as an accompaniment or entrée

Per serving: 166 calories, 6 g protein, 23 g carbohydrate, 6 g total fat (1 g saturated), 0 mg cholesterol, 353 mg sodium, 239 mg potassium

Preparation Time: 25 minutes
Cooking Time: 15 minutes

45

INGREDIENTS

5	OZ/155 G DRIED VERMICELLI *OR* CAPELLINI, BROKEN INTO 1/2-IN/12-MM PIECES
2	OZ/60 G CHOPPED ONION
1	CLOVE GARLIC, THINLY SLICED
2	TABLESPOONS OLIVE OIL *OR* COOKING OIL
2	TOMATOES, PEELED, SEEDED, AND CHOPPED
16	FL OZ/500 ML CHICKEN STOCK
3	SMALL FRESH CHILIES, SEEDED AND THINLY SLICED
1/2	TEASPOON DRIED OREGANO, CRUSHED
1/4	TEASPOON GROUND CUMIN
1/4	TEASPOON SALT
2	TABLESPOONS CHOPPED FRESH CORIANDER
	CHOPPED FRESH TOMATOES (OPTIONAL)

In this unusual preparation, the vermicelli is first sautéed in oil, then cooked with the rest of the sauce.

Spaghetti & Meatballs

INGREDIENTS

	CLASSIC TOMATO SAUCE (PAGE 18)
1	BEATEN EGG
1-1/2	OZ/45 G SOFT BREAD CRUMBS
1	OZ/30 G FINELY CHOPPED ONION
2	TABLESPOONS FINELY CHOPPED GREEN PEPPER (CAPSICUM)
1/4	TEASPOON SALT
1/4	TEASPOON DRIED OREGANO, CRUSHED
1	LB/500 G LEAN MINCED BEEF OR PORK SAUSAGE MEAT
1	TABLESPOON COOKING OIL
8	OZ/250 G DRIED SPAGHETTI OR LINGUINE OR 1 LB/500 G FRESH LINGUINE OR OTHER RIBBON PASTA

Preparation Time: 1 hour (includes sauce)
Cooking Time: 21 to 27 minutes

STEPS AT A GLANCE	Page
MAKING PASTA	8–14
CUTTING RIBBON PASTA	28
MAKING TOMATO SAUCE	18

*I*f you prefer not to brown the meatballs in a frying pan, you can bake them in a preheated 375°F/190°C oven for about 20 minutes, or till no pink remains. To make soft bread crumbs, shred the bread with a fork or process briefly in a blender or food processor.

■ Prepare classic tomato sauce as directed; keep warm.

■ In a large mixing bowl combine egg, bread crumbs, onion, green pepper, salt, and oregano. Add beef or sausage meat; mix well. Shape into thirty 1-in/2.5-cm meatballs. In a large frying pan heat the oil and cook the meatballs, in 2 batches, for 8 to 10 minutes, or till no pink remains. Drain well. Add meatballs to the warm sauce. Cook, uncovered, for 5 minutes to heat through and blend flavours, stirring occasionally. Keep warm.

■ In a large saucepan or pasta pot bring 3 qt/3 l water to boiling. Add pasta. Reduce heat slightly. Boil, uncovered, 8 to 12 minutes for dried pasta or 1½ to 2 minutes for fresh, or till al dente, stirring occasionally. (Or, cook according to package directions.) Drain immediately.

■ Serve sauce and meatballs over hot pasta.

Serves 4 to 6 as a main course

Per serving: 681 calories, 34 g protein, 73 g carbohydrate, 29 g total fat (8 g saturated), 123 mg cholesterol, 564 mg sodium, 1,372 mg potassium

46

Everyone's favourite pasta dish: tasty meatballs in a simple tomato sauce on a bed of spaghetti. Sprinkle with Parmesan if desired.

Linguine with Spicy Chili Sauce & Beans

INGREDIENTS

8	OZ/250 G DRIED LINGUINE *OR* SPAGHETTI *OR* 1 LB/500 G FRESH LINGUINE *OR* OTHER RIBBON PASTA

MEAT SAUCE

1	LB/500 G RIPE PLUM (ROMA) TOMATOES *OR* TINNED TOMATOES, CUT UP, WITH JUICE
1	LB/500 G LEAN MINCED CHICKEN, TURKEY, *OR* BEEF
2	OZ/60 G CHOPPED ONION
1	CLOVE GARLIC, MINCED
8	OZ/250 G TINNED *OR* BOTTLED ITALIAN-STYLE TOMATO SAUCE
2	FL OZ/60 ML CHICKEN STOCK
1	TABLESPOON RED WINE VINEGAR
1	TABLESPOON CHILI POWDER
1/2	TEASPOON GROUND ALLSPICE
1/4	TEASPOON GROUND CINNAMON
1/4	TEASPOON SALT
1/8	TEASPOON GROUND RED PEPPER (CAYENNE) (OPTIONAL)

TOPPINGS

16	OZ/500 G TINNED CANNELLINI BEANS
1	OZ/30 G THINLY SLICED SPRING ONIONS
2	OZ/60 G SHREDDED CHEDDAR CHEESE *OR* 1 OZ/30 G GRATED PARMESAN CHEESE

Preparation Time: 30 minutes
Cooking Time: 20 to 25 minutes

*I*f you ordered this dish in the American Midwest, it would be called "five-way" chili because it contains pasta, chili, cheese, onions, and beans.

■ In a large saucepan or pasta pot bring 3 qt/3 l water to boiling. Add pasta. Reduce heat slightly. Boil, uncovered, for 8 to 12 minutes for dried pasta or 1½ to 2 minutes for fresh, or till al dente, stirring occasionally. Drain immediately.

■ Meanwhile, peel, seed, and chop fresh plum tomatoes, if using. In a large frying pan cook minced chicken, turkey, or beef, onion, and garlic for 5 minutes, or till meat is brown and onion is tender. Drain off fat. Stir in fresh or undrained tinned tomatoes, tomato sauce, chicken stock, vinegar, chili powder, allspice, cinnamon, salt, and, if desired, red pepper. Bring to boiling; reduce heat. Simmer, uncovered, for 15 to 20 minutes, or to desired consistency, stirring occasionally.

■ To serve, heat cannellini beans in a small saucepan; drain. Top hot cooked pasta with meat sauce, beans, spring onions, and Cheddar or Parmesan cheese. Serve immediately.

Serves 4 to 6 as a main course

Per serving: 530 calories, 36 g protein, 74 g carbohydrate, 13 g total fat (5 g saturated), 69 mg cholesterol, 866 mg sodium, 993 mg potassium

This surprising version of pasta and meat sauce features the bold flavours of chili.

STEPS AT A GLANCE	Page
MAKING PASTA	8–14
CUTTING RIBBON PASTA	28
PREPARING SAUCE INGREDIENTS	16
SIMMERING SAUCE	18

47

Stir-fried Vegetables with Buckwheat Noodles

Preparation Time: 30 minutes
Cooking Time: 16 to 17 minutes

Soba noodles, made from buckwheat, are a favourite in Japan and are enjoyed either hot or cold.

STEPS AT A GLANCE	Page
COOKING PASTA	12

INGREDIENTS

4	OZ/125 G DRIED BUCKWHEAT NOODLES (SOBA), CHINESE EGG NOODLES, *OR* FINE EGG NOODLES

SAUCE

4	FL OZ/125 ML CHICKEN STOCK
1	TABLESPOON CORNFLOUR
1	TABLESPOON SOY SAUCE
2	TEASPOONS SESAME OIL

VEGETABLES

1	TABLESPOON COOKING OIL
10	OZ/315 G EXTRA-FIRM TOFU, DRAINED AND CUT INTO THIN STRIPS
2	TEASPOONS GRATED FRESH GINGER ROOT
2	CLOVES GARLIC, CUT INTO SLIVERS (1 TEASPOON)
1	RED *OR* YELLOW PEPPER (CAPSICUM), CUT INTO THIN STRIPS
3	OZ/90 G FRESH SNOW PEAS (MANGETOUT)
5	OZ/155 G SLICED YELLOW BABY SQUASH *OR* COURGETTES
3	SPRING ONIONS, BIAS-SLICED INTO 1-IN/2.5-CM PIECES

*P*asta is wonderfully versatile: it's not just for meals with an Italian accent, as you'll see when you taste this Asian-style dish.

■ In a large saucepan or pasta pot bring 3 qt/3 l water to boiling. Add buckwheat noodles or egg noodles. Reduce heat slightly. Boil, uncovered, 10 minutes for buckwheat noodles or 4 to 6 minutes for egg noodles, or till al dente, stirring occasionally. (Or, cook according to package directions.) Drain immediately.

■ Meanwhile, for sauce, in a small mixing bowl stir together chicken stock, cornflour, soy sauce, and sesame oil; set aside.

■ For vegetables, in a large frying pan heat cooking oil over medium-high heat. Add tofu, ginger, and garlic. Cook for 2 minutes, or till tofu is heated through, turning tofu once. Remove from pan. Add red or yellow pepper, yellow baby squash or courgettes, and spring onions to skillet. Stir-fry for 2 to 3 minutes, or till crisp-tender. Push vegetables to sides of pan. Stir sauce and add to centre of pan. Cook and stir till thickened and bubbly. Return tofu and noodles to pan. Stir all ingredients together to coat with sauce; heat through and serve immediately.

Serves 4 as a main course

Per serving: 231 calories, 13 g protein, 31 g carbohydrate, 8 g total fat (1 g saturated), 0 mg cholesterol, 602 mg sodium, 380 mg potassium

Szechwan Chicken & Pasta

Preparation Time: 25 minutes
Cooking Time: 11 to 13 minutes

INGREDIENTS

1	LB/500 G BONELESS, SKINLESS CHICKEN BREASTS
6	OZ/185 G FRESH SNOW PEAS (MANGETOUT)
2	FL OZ/60 ML SOY SAUCE
2	TABLESPOONS RICE VINEGAR OR WHITE WINE VINEGAR
1	TEASPOON CHILI OIL OR SESAME OIL WITH 1/8 TEASPOON CHILI POWDER
1/4	TO 1/2 TEASPOON CRUSHED RED PEPPER (CHILI) FLAKES
5	OZ/155 G DRIED CHINESE EGG NOODLES OR 8 OZ/250 G FRESH CHINESE EGG NOODLES
1	TABLESPOON COOKING OIL
2	CLOVES GARLIC, MINCED
1	LARGE RED OR GREEN PEPPER (CAPSICUM), CUT INTO THIN STRIPS
2	SPRING ONIONS, SLICED
1-1/2	OZ/45 G COARSELY CHOPPED PEANUTS

*C*hinese egg noodles are made from wheat flour, water, and egg and are shaped either round or flat. They are available fresh or dried. Many well-stocked supermarkets carry fresh noodles in the refrigerator together with spring-roll wrappers. You can substitute any fresh ribbon pasta for the fresh Chinese noodles, if you prefer.

■ Rinse chicken and pat dry. Cut into ¾-in/2-cm pieces. Coarsely chop the snow peas. In a small bowl stir together the soy sauce, vinegar, chili oil, and crushed red pepper. Set aside.

■ For dried noodles, in a large saucepan or pasta pot bring 3 qt/3 l water to boiling. Add noodles. Reduce heat slightly. Boil, uncovered, 4 to 6 minutes, or till tender, stirring occasionally. (Prepare fresh noodles according to package directions.) Drain.

■ Pour cooking oil into a wok or large frying pan. (Add more oil as necessary during cooking.) Preheat over medium-high heat. Stir-fry the garlic in hot oil for 15 seconds. Add the snow peas, red or green pepper, and spring onions; stir-fry for 1 to 2 minutes, or till crisp-tender. Remove the vegetables from the wok.

■ Add half the chicken to the hot wok. Stir-fry for 2 to 3 minutes, or till no pink remains. Remove the chicken from the wok. Repeat with remaining chicken. Return all chicken to the wok. Add the soy sauce mixture to the wok. Add the cooked vegetables and noodles. Stir ingredients together to coat with soy sauce mixture. Cook and stir about 1 minute more, or till heated through. Sprinkle with peanuts. Serve immediately.

Serves 5 as a main course

Per serving: 369 calories, 27 g protein, 39 g carbohydrate, 12 g total fat (2 g saturated), 87 mg cholesterol, 910 mg sodium, 407 mg potassium

49

This pasta meal is full of healthy vegetables, low-fat chicken, and a tangy mixture of soy sauce, chili oil, and rice vinegar.

Filipino-Style Noodles

INGREDIENTS

2	OZ/60 G CHOPPED ONION
2	CLOVES GARLIC, MINCED
2	TABLESPOONS COOKING OIL
4	OZ/125 G THINLY BIAS-SLICED CARROTS
1	SMALL ZUCCHINI (COURGETTE), CUT INTO SHORT, THIN STRIPS
3	OZ/90 G SHREDDED CABBAGE
8	FL OZ/250 ML CHICKEN STOCK
2	TABLESPOONS SOY SAUCE
5	OZ/155 G COOKED PORK, SLICED INTO THIN STRIPS
5	OZ/155 G COOKED PRAWNS, CHOPPED
8	OZ/250 G PANCIT CANTON NOODLES OR DRIED CHINESE EGG NOODLES
1	OZ/30 G SLICED SPRING ONIONS

Preparation Time: 25 minutes
Cooking Time: 12 minutes

STEPS AT A GLANCE	Page
PREPARING SAUCE INGREDIENTS	16

*P*ancit canton noodles are a favourite in the Philippines, where pancit means "noodle." Because they are pre-cooked and sold dried, they need only be added to boiling liquid for a brief time before they are tender.

■ In a 12-in/30-cm frying pan cook onion and garlic in hot oil for 5 minutes, or till tender but not brown. Add carrots, zucchini (courgette), cabbage, chicken stock, and soy sauce; mix well. Bring to boiling; reduce heat. Cover and simmer for 5 minutes, or till carrots are crisp-tender. Stir in pork and prawns.

■ Break noodles apart and stir into cooked mixture. (If necessary, add additional chicken stock to cook noodles.) Cover and cook over low heat about 2 minutes for pancit canton noodles and 4 to 6 minutes for egg noodles, or till noodles are tender and liquid is absorbed. Stir mixture gently and transfer to a serving dish. If desired, sprinkle with spring onions.

Serves 4 as a main course

Per serving: 407 calories, 22 g protein, 51 g carbohydrate,
12 g total fat (3 g saturated), 79 mg cholesterol,
1,861 mg sodium, 553 mg potassium

50

This stir-fry dish contains the
same ingredients as egg roll
stuffing, but here they are served
with long wheat noodles.

Shaped Pasta

Steps in Making Shaped Pasta

Cut basic rectangles and circles for shaping from pasta dough with a fluted pastry wheel and a ruler, or a round biscuit cutter.

BISCUIT CUTTER

CUTTING BOARD

FLUTED PASTRY
WHEEL

RULER

52

ONLY A VERY FEW of the hundreds of charming pasta shapes that are turned out so effortlessly in the factory can be formed by hand.

Farfalle, which to some resemble little butterflies and to others bow ties, may be the easiest to do. They begin as small rectangles of dough cut from a freshly rolled sheet. If you prefer them with a decoratively pinked edge, use a fluted pastry wheel to cut them. Otherwise, any sharp knife or a straight-edge pizza cutter will work well.

Tripolini are also described as bow ties, but rather than having crisp, straight edges and sharp, angular corners, they are rounded like the bow ties worn by circus clowns. They are formed in the same way as farfalle, but begin as circles rather than rectangles.

Orecchiette are thin cups said to have originated in Apulia, an Italian region that makes up the heel of Italy's boot. This is a wonderful pasta for sauces because it not only absorbs the sauce, but traps it inside the cup.

For any of these shapes, prepare Homemade Pasta dough, page 14, as directed, then follow the steps on the opposite page. Let the shaped pasta dry partially on a flour-dusted towel or baking sheet before cooking, or dry it completely if storing in the refrigerator. Turn occasionally to expose both sides to the air.

Homemade farfalle and tripolini will cook in 2 to 3 minutes. Orecchiette are thicker and take a little more time, 6 to 7 minutes. All three are available as packaged dried pastas, too. These pastas are delicious served hot with meat and vegetable sauces. Florentine-inspired Chicken Livers over Pasta, page 66, features chicken livers and farfalle or tripolini in a creamy sauce dotted with colourful bits of red and green peppers. Orecchiette with Fennel in Parmesan Cream, page 68, is an anise-flavoured combination of fresh fennel and Sambuca plus mushrooms and Italian prosciutto ham. These shapes are attractive additions to pasta salads as well. Warm Tomato–Feta Cheese Salad, page 115, is a refreshing summer dish that shows off farfalle — either fresh or dried.

you can also use a pizza wheel or a knife to cut the strips

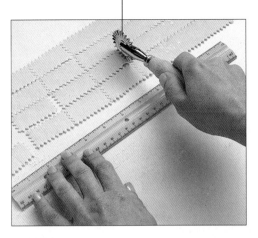

if the pasta is too dry to hold the pinch, dab a little water in the centre

save and reroll dough scraps to make more pasta

STEP 1 MAKING FARFALLE (BOW TIES)

Roll the dough ¹⁄₁₆ in/2 mm thick and trim the sides so that they are straight and even. Using a fluted pastry wheel, cut the dough into 1-in/2.5-cm-wide strips. Then cut crosswise every 2 in/5 cm to form 2x1-in/5x2.5-cm rectangles.

STEP 2 SHAPING FARFALLE

To form the bow tie, pinch the centre of the rectangle. To create a nice fold, first lay your index finger or little finger sideways in the centre of the dough and pinch against it. Remove your finger and finish making the pinch.

STEP 3 MAKING TRIPOLINI

Using a 1-in or 1¼-in/2.5-cm or 3-cm round cutter, cut the dough into circles. Shape as for farfalle (step 2): Pinch the centre of each circle to form a rounded bow tie.

53

don't flour the work surface or the dough too heavily or the log will slide instead of rolling

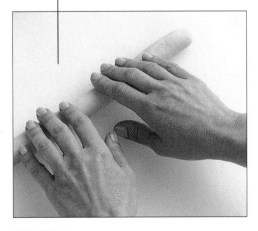

flour your hands as needed to keep the pasta from sticking

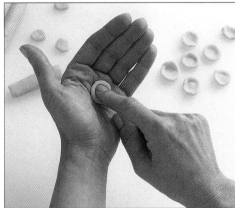

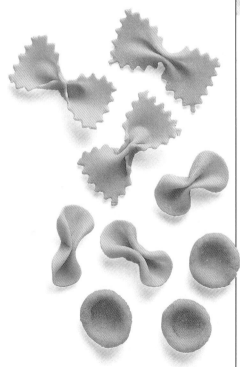

STEP 4 MAKING ORECCHIETTE

Shape 4 to 6 oz/125 to 185 g of pasta dough into a log ½ in/12 mm in diameter. Roll with even pressure to avoid denting the dough and to keep it uniformly thick.

STEP 5 SHAPING ORECCHIETTE

With a sharp knife, slice the roll into ⅛-in/3-mm-thick slices. Place one slice in your palm. Shape it into a little cup by pressing the middle of the slice with your index finger. Twist your finger to broaden the cup.

Whimsical pasta shapes like far-falle (bow ties), tripolini (rounded bow ties), and orecchiette ("little ears") are easily formed by hand.

Dried Shaped Pasta

NOWHERE IS THE PLAYFUL side of the Italian character better illustrated than in the myriad shapes of dried pasta offered by commercial manufacturers. There are literally hundreds. Where else but in Italy would you eat food that looks like little radiators (radiatori) and corkscrews (fusilli), thimbles (ditali) and shells (conchiglie), bow ties (farfalle) and little ears (orecchiette), wheels (ruote) and rice or barley (orzo)! Often the same shape appears in several sizes (the smaller often ends in *ini* or *etti*, which are diminutives). For example, ditali are tubes about ½ in/12 mm long; ditalini are shorter. The same shape may be called one thing in one region and another elsewhere. One name can even be applied to more than one shape! Confusing, yes. A problem, not at all. Most shapes are interchangeable.

Dried shaped pasta complements sauces with large pieces of vegetables, similar in size to the pasta. Shells, spirals, and rigatoni go with meaty sauces because their indentations trap bits of ingredients. Small shells, elbow macaroni, and tubular ditali are good in soups.

to use with a sauce, cook shaped pasta in boiling water as shown on pages 12 and 13

STEP 1 ADDING PASTA TO BOILING STOCK

Bring a large pot of tasty stock to a rolling boil. Add pasta to the stock gradually, so that it keeps boiling. The pasta will absorb much of the cooking liquid, so be sure to use a generous amount of stock.

54

Dried pasta is available in a delightful array of shapes, including elbows, bow ties, wheels, tubes, and shells.

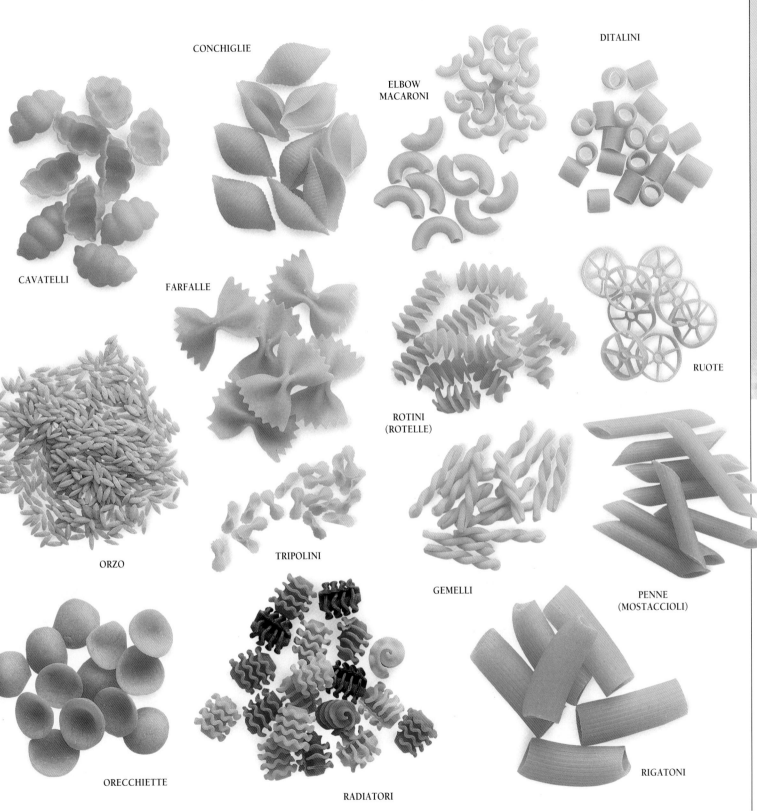

CONCHIGLIE

ELBOW
MACARONI

DITALINI

CAVATELLI

FARFALLE

RUOTE

ROTINI
(ROTELLE)

ORZO

TRIPOLINI

GEMELLI

PENNE
(MOSTACCIOLI)

ORECCHIETTE

RADIATORI

RIGATONI

Pasta & Prawns in Asparagus Sauce

Preparation Time: 30 minutes
Cooking Time: 15 minutes

INGREDIENTS

12	OZ/375 G FRESH OR FROZEN PRAWNS, PEELED AND DEVEINED
1-1/2	LB/750 G FRESH ASPARAGUS SPEARS
8	OZ/250 G GEMELLI, ROTINI, OR OTHER DRIED SHAPED PASTA
8	FL OZ/250 ML CHICKEN STOCK
2	FL OZ/60 G SOUR CREAM
2	TABLESPOONS PLAIN FLOUR
1/4	TEASPOON SALT
1/8	TEASPOON WHITE PEPPER
1	TABLESPOON LEMON JUICE

*W*hen setting aside asparagus pieces before puréeing, choose only the tips, which are usually the most tender part of the stalk and the most attractive.

■ Thaw prawns, if frozen. Snap off and discard woody asparagus bases. Cut spears into 1½-in/4-cm pieces. Cook, covered, in a small amount of boiling water for 6 to 8 minutes, or till crisp-tender. Drain, reserving 2 fl oz/60 ml of the cooking liquid. Set aside 4 oz/125 g of the asparagus pieces; keep warm. In a blender container or food processor bowl, purée remaining asparagus with the reserved cooking liquid till nearly smooth.

■ Meanwhile, in a large saucepan or pasta pot bring 3 qt/3 l water to boiling. Add pasta. Reduce heat slightly. Boil, uncovered, for 8 to 10 minutes. Add prawns to boiling pasta during the last 3 minutes of cooking. Cook till pasta is al dente and prawns turn pink, stirring occasionally. (Or, cook according to package directions, adding prawns for the last 3 minutes.) Drain immediately. Return pasta and prawns to warm pan; add asparagus pieces.

■ In a medium saucepan stir together chicken stock, sour cream, flour, salt, and pepper. Add asparagus purée and lemon juice. Cook and stir over medium heat till thickened and bubbly. Cook and stir for 1 minute more. Pour sauce over hot pasta mixture and toss to coat. Serve immediately.

Serves 4 as a main course

Per serving: 356 calories, 24 g protein, 53 g carbohydrate, 5 g total fat (2 g saturated), 116 mg cholesterol, 465 mg sodium, 497 mg potassium

56

STEPS IN MAKING ASPARAGUS SAUCE

STEP 1 PREPARING ASPARAGUS
Hold the asparagus stalk in both hands and press with your thumbs toward the thicker end. Snap off the woody base and discard.

STEP 2 MAKING PURÉE
Cook asparagus pieces in boiling water until crisp-tender. Blend all but 4 oz/125 g with the reserved cooking water in a blender or food processor to a chunky purée.

When asparagus makes its long-awaited appearance in the spring, use the delicate vegetable to make this elegant main course.

Artichokes and lamb combine in a Greek-
inspired sauce served over tiny pasta
that resembles grains of barley.

58

Artichokes, Lamb & Orzo Avgolemono

INGREDIENTS

2	TABLESPOONS OLIVE OIL *OR* COOKING OIL
1	LB/500 G BONELESS LEAN LAMB, CUT INTO 3/4-IN/2-CM CUBES
4	OZ/125 G CHOPPED ONION
1	GARLIC CLOVE, MINCED
6	FL OZ/185 G WHITE WINE *OR* CHICKEN STOCK
1-1/2	TEASPOONS CHOPPED FRESH OREGANO *OR* 1/2 TEASPOON DRIED OREGANO, CRUSHED
1	TEASPOON FINELY SHREDDED LEMON PEEL
1/4	TEASPOON SALT
1/4	TEASPOON PEPPER
6	FRESH MEDIUM ARTICHOKES, TRIMMED, HALVED, AND BLANCHED, *OR* 9 OZ/280 G FROZEN ARTICHOKE HEARTS
8	OZ/250 G ORZO
1	BEATEN EGG
2	TABLESPOONS LEMON JUICE
1	TABLESPOON CORNFLOUR
4	FL OZ/125 ML WARM CHICKEN STOCK
2	TABLESPOONS CHOPPED FRESH PARSLEY (OPTIONAL)

*A*vgolemono, a Greek sauce made with lemon juice and egg, is the base for this Mediterranean-style lamb and artichoke topping for orzo pasta. Try leg of lamb, fillet, or shoulder for lean cuts of lamb.

■ In a cooking pot or large frying pan heat the oil and brown half the lamb; remove meat. Brown remaining meat with onion and garlic till onion is tender. Drain fat from all the meat. Return all the meat to pan. Stir in 6 fl oz/185 ml wine or chicken stock, oregano, lemon peel, salt, and pepper. Bring to boiling; reduce heat. Cover; simmer for 20 minutes. Add artichokes and simmer 10 minutes more, or till tender.

■ Meanwhile, in a large saucepan or pasta pot bring 3 qt/3 l water to boiling. Add pasta. Reduce heat slightly. Boil, uncovered, for 5 to 8 minutes, or till al dente, stirring occasionally. (Or, cook according to package directions.) Drain immediately. Return to warm pan; keep warm.

■ In a small mixing bowl combine egg, lemon juice, cornflour, and 4 fl oz/125 ml warm chicken stock. Pour egg mixture into the lamb-artichoke mixture. Cook and stir over medium heat for 1 minute, or till thickened and bubbly. Cook and stir for 2 minutes more. Serve lamb mixture over hot cooked pasta. If desired, garnish with parsley.

Serves 4 as a main course

Per serving: 525 calories, 31 g protein, 61 g carbohydrate, 15 g total fat (3 g saturated), 111 mg cholesterol, 356 mg sodium, 661 mg potassium

Preparation Time: 20 minutes
Cooking Time: 45 minutes

STEPS AT A GLANCE	Page
PREPARING ARTICHOKES	59
PREPARING SAUCE INGREDIENTS	16
COOKING PASTA	12

STEPS IN PREPARING ARTICHOKES

STEP 1 TRIMMING ARTICHOKES

Trim stem flush with bottom. Break off tough outer leaves until only soft ones with a tinge of yellow remain.

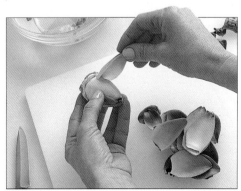

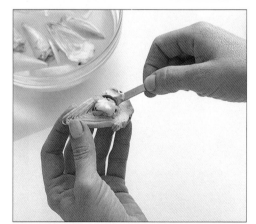

STEP 2 REMOVING CHOKES

Trim leaves to about 1 in/2.5 cm long. Cut artichoke in half to expose the choke. Scoop out the hairy choke with a tiny spoon or a melon baller and discard.

STEP 3 ADDING HEARTS TO WATER

Fill a bowl with water and squeeze some lemon juice into it, then drop in the lemon slices. To prevent browning, float trimmed pieces in acidulated water until needed.

Stuffed Peppers with Orzo

Preparation Time: 20 minutes
Baking Time: 15 minutes

INGREDIENTS

2	LARGE RED, YELLOW, *AND/OR* GREEN PEPPERS (CAPSICUMS)
12	OZ/375 G GROUND (MINCED) LAMB, TURKEY, *OR* PORK
1	OZ/30 G CHOPPED ONION
8	OZ/250 G TINNED ITALIAN-STYLE TOMATOES, CHOPPED
2	OZ/60 G ORZO
1	TABLESPOON CHOPPED FRESH MINT, BASIL, *OR* OREGANO, *OR* 1/2 TEASPOON DRIED MINT, BASIL, *OR* OREGANO, CRUSHED
1/2	TEASPOON GROUND ALLSPICE
4	FL OZ/125 ML WATER
1/4	TEASPOON SALT
1/4	TEASPOON PEPPER
2	OZ/60 G GRATED PARMESAN CHEESE

*O*rzo is a barley-shaped pasta frequently used in recipes as a substitute for rice. Here it cooks in the stuffing mixture, saving the step of cooking the pasta separately.

■ Halve peppers lengthwise, removing stem ends, seeds, and membranes. Immerse peppers in boiling water for 3 minutes. Remove and sprinkle insides with salt. Invert peppers on paper towels to drain well.

■ In a frying pan cook lamb, turkey, or pork and onion for 5 minutes, or till meat is brown and onion is tender. Drain fat. Stir in tomatoes, uncooked pasta, mint, basil, or oregano, allspice, water, salt, and pepper. Bring to boiling; reduce heat. Cover and simmer for 7 to 8 minutes, or till pasta is al dente. Stir in 1 oz/30 g of the Parmesan cheese. Fill peppers with meat mixture.

■ Place in a 2-qt/2-l square baking dish with any remaining meat mixture. Bake in a preheated 375°F/190°C oven for about 15 minutes, or till heated through. Sprinkle with remaining cheese. Let stand for 1 to 2 minutes before serving.

Serves 4 as a main course

Per serving: 327 calories, 24 g protein, 22 g carbohydrate, 16 g total fat (8 g saturated), 68 mg cholesterol, 458 mg sodium, 509 mg potassium

STEPS AT A GLANCE	Page
PREPARING SAUCE INGREDIENTS	16
STUFFING PEPPERS	60

60

STEPS IN STUFFING PEPPERS

STEP 1 **DRAINING PEPPERS**
Drop stemmed and seeded pepper halves in boiling water for several minutes to soften. Remove from the water with tongs, sprinkle the insides with salt, and drain on paper towels, cut-side down.

STEP 2 **STUFFING PEPPERS**
Prepare the meat mixture, add the orzo, and cook until tender. Add cheese. Turn the peppers cut-side up. Spoon one quarter of the filling into each pepper half. Transfer to a baking dish.

Stuff colourful peppers with a Middle
Eastern filling of spice-scented
minced lamb and orzo instead
of the usual rice.

62

The sunny flavours and colours of
the Mediterranean are captured
in this sauce.

Pasta with Tapenade

**Preparation Time: 20 minutes
Cooking Time: 12 to 14 minutes**

INGREDIENTS

8	OZ/250 G CAVATELLI, CONCHIGLIE, OR OTHER DRIED SHAPED PASTA
1/2	A FENNEL BULB OR 2 OZ/60 G CELERY, BIAS-SLICED 1/4 IN/6 MM THICK
1/2	A RED PEPPER (CAPSICUM), CUT INTO THIN BITE-SIZE STRIPS
1/2	A YELLOW PEPPER (CAPSICUM), CUT INTO THIN BITE-SIZE STRIPS
4	OZ/125 G PITTED BLACK GREEK OLIVES, NIÇOISE OLIVES, OR PITTED RIPE OLIVES
3-1/2	OZ/105 G TUNA, TINNED IN WATER, DRAINED
1	TABLESPOON CAPERS, DRAINED
1/2	TEASPOON DRIED OREGANO OR THYME, CRUSHED
1	TEASPOON ANCHOVY PASTE (OPTIONAL)
1	CLOVE GARLIC
1	TABLESPOON OLIVE OIL OR COOKING OIL
1	TO 2 TEASPOONS LEMON JUICE
2	TABLESPOONS CHOPPED FRESH PARSLEY

*T*apenade, a purée of olives, capers, and anchovies, is generally offered as an appetiser served with bread, but it also makes a splendid main course when tossed with hot pasta.

■ In a large saucepan or pasta pot bring 3 qt/3 l water to boiling. Add pasta. Reduce heat slightly. Boil, uncovered, for 12 to 14 minutes, or till pasta is al dente, stirring occasionally. Add fennel and red and yellow peppers during the last 2 minutes of cooking. (Or, cook according to package directions, adding fennel and peppers for the last 2 minutes.) Drain immediately. Return pasta-vegetable mixture to warm pan.

■ Meanwhile, in a food processor bowl or blender container place the olives, tuna, capers, oregano or thyme, anchovy paste (if desired), garlic, and oil. Process or blend till mixture is smooth. Add lemon juice to taste. Add tuna mixture and parsley to hot cooked pasta mixture and toss to coat. Serve immediately.

Serves 4 as a main dish

Per serving: 315 calories, 15 g protein, 49 g carbohydrate, 8 g total fat (1 g saturated), 4 mg cholesterol, 138 mg sodium, 187 mg potassium

STEPS IN PREPARING FENNEL

STEP 1 CUTTING FENNEL

Trim away the feathery stalks just above where the bulb begins. Leave the root end on. If necessary, remove any damaged outer stalks.

STEP 2 SLICING FENNEL

Cut the trimmed bulb in half. Rinse between the layers to remove any grit. Lay one half on a cutting board, cut-side down. Cut into 1/4-in/6-mm-thick slices with a sharp knife.

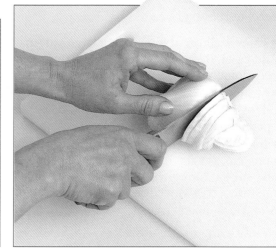

Scallops & Penne in Red Sauce

Long, narrow tubes of penne provide an attractive visual contrast to rounds of succulent scallops and bits of fresh tomato.

Preparation Time: 30 minutes
Cooking Time: 20 minutes

INGREDIENTS

12	OZ/375 G FRESH *OR* FROZEN SCALLOPS
8	OZ/250 G PENNE, RIGATONI, *OR* OTHER DRIED SHAPED PASTA
2	CLOVES GARLIC, MINCED
2	TABLESPOONS OLIVE OIL *OR* COOKING OIL
4	OZ/125 G VERMOUTH *OR* RED WINE
2	TEASPOONS CORNFLOUR
2	LB/1 KG RIPE PLUM (ROMA) TOMATOES, PEELED, SEEDED, AND FINELY CHOPPED
4	OZ/125 G BOTTLED DICED PIMIENTO, DRAINED
2	TABLESPOONS CHOPPED FRESH PARSLEY
2	TABLESPOONS CHOPPED FRESH BASIL
1/2	TEASPOON SALT
1/4	TEASPOON CRUSHED RED PEPPER (CHILI) FLAKES
1	OZ/30 G GRATED PARMESAN CHEESE (OPTIONAL)

64

W*atch the scallops carefully as they cook, and remove them the second they become opaque, or they will quickly become rubbery.*

■ Thaw scallops, if frozen. In a large saucepan or pasta pot bring 3 qt/3 l water to boiling. Add pasta. Reduce heat slightly. Boil, uncovered, for 14 to 15 minutes, or till al dente, stirring occasionally. (Or, cook according to package directions.) Drain immediately.

■ Meanwhile, halve the scallops, if large. In a large frying pan cook and stir the garlic in hot oil for 1 minute. Add the scallops. Cook and stir for 2 minutes more, or till scallops are opaque. Remove scallops from pan; keep warm.

■ In the frying pan stir together the vermouth or red wine and cornflour. Stir in tomatoes, pimiento, parsley, basil, salt, and red pepper. Cook and stir till thickened and bubbly. Cook and stir for 2 minutes more. Add hot cooked pasta and scallops and toss to coat with tomato mixture. Serve immediately with Parmesan cheese, if desired.

Serves 4 as a main course

Per serving: 409 calories, 20 g protein, 55 g carbohydrate, 9 g total fat (1 g saturated), 25 mg cholesterol, 417 mg sodium, 651 mg potassium

STEPS AT A GLANCE	Page
PREPARING SAUCE INGREDIENTS	16
COOKING PASTA	12

Pesto Pasta with Vegetables

*B*ring the pesto to room temperature if you've had it stored in the refrigerator or freezer. Or, substitute purchased pesto for homemade.

■ Prepare pesto as directed. Set aside.

■ Cut potatoes into halves if very small or into bite-size pieces. Cut green beans into 2-in/5-cm pieces. In a medium saucepan cook potatoes and green beans in a small amount of boiling salted water for about 10 minutes, or till vegetables are tender. Drain well.

■ Meanwhile, in a large saucepan or pasta pot bring 3 qt/3 l water to boiling. Add pasta. Reduce heat slightly. Boil, uncovered, for 8 to 12 minutes, or till al dente, stirring occasionally. (Or, cook according to package directions.) Drain immediately. Return pasta to warm pan. Add potatoes and green beans.

■ In a small mixing bowl stir together pesto and enough of the water to make a sauce consistency. Pour the pesto mixture and Parmesan cheese over the pasta and vegetables and toss to coat. Serve immediately.

Serves 4 as an accompaniment or entrée

Per serving: 274 calories, 10 g protein, 40 g carbohydrate, 9 g total fat (2 g saturated), 7 mg cholesterol, 154 mg sodium, 471 mg potassium

INGREDIENTS

2	FL OZ/60 ML PESTO (PAGE 22)
8	OZ/250 G WHOLE TINY NEW POTATOES
6	OZ/185 G GREEN BEANS
4	OZ/125 G RADIATORI, ROTINI, *OR* OTHER DRIED SHAPED PASTA
1	TO 2 TABLESPOONS WATER
2	TABLESPOONS GRATED PARMESAN CHEESE

Preparation Time: 35 minutes (includes pesto)
Cooking Time: 8 to 12 minutes

STEPS AT A GLANCE	**Page**
MAKING PESTO	22
COOKING PASTA	12

65

When you bite into crinkly radiatori, they release a burst of the sauce trapped in their deep folds.

Chicken Livers over Pasta

*I*talian cooks, particularly Florentines, adore chicken livers. One of the many good culinary uses to which they put them is this rich and hearty sauce for pasta. They're served with shaped pasta so that you can pick up a delicious morsel of liver with each bite.

■ In a large saucepan or pasta pot bring 3 qt/3 l water to boiling. Add pasta. Reduce heat slightly. Boil, uncovered, 10 minutes for dried farfalle (5 to 6 minutes for dried tripolini) or 2 to 3 minutes for fresh, or till al dente, stirring occasionally. (Or, cook according to package directions.) Drain immediately. Return pasta to warm pan.

■ Meanwhile, in a large frying pan cook chicken livers in hot margarine or butter over medium-high heat, turning as needed, for 4 to 5 minutes, or till centres are just slightly pink. Remove from pan; keep warm. Reserve pan drippings.

■ In the same pan cook the spring onion and green and red peppers in the pan drippings for 2 to 3 minutes, or till tender. Stir in flour, salt, and pepper. Add chicken stock, light cream or milk, and sage. Cook and stir till thickened and bubbly. Cook and stir for 1 minute more. Pour sauce over hot cooked pasta and toss to coat. Add chicken livers; toss gently. Serve immediately.

Serves 4 as a main course

Per serving: 475 calories, 24 g protein, 53 g carbohydrate, 18 g total fat (7 g saturated), 359 mg cholesterol, 503 mg sodium, 290 mg potassium

Dress up chicken livers by serving them with pasta shaped like little bow ties.

Preparation Time: 25 minutes
Cooking Time: 10 minutes

INGREDIENTS

8	OZ/250 G DRIED *OR* 16 OZ/500 G FRESH FARFALLE *OR* TRIPOLINI
12	OZ/375 G CHICKEN LIVERS, CUT IN HALF
2	TABLESPOONS MARGARINE *OR* BUTTER
1	OZ/30 G SLICED SPRING ONION
1-1/2	OZ/45 G CHOPPED GREEN PEPPER (CAPSICUM)
1-1/2	OZ/45 G CHOPPED RED PEPPER (CAPSICUM)
2	OZ/60 G PLAIN FLOUR
1/4	TEASPOON SALT
1/4	TEASPOON PEPPER
10	FL OZ/315 ML CHICKEN STOCK
5	FL OZ/160 ML LIGHT (SINGLE) CREAM *OR* MILK
1	TABLESPOON CHOPPED FRESH SAGE

Piselli e Pasta (Peas & Pasta)

Inspired by a Venetian classic made
with peas and rice, this seasoned pasta
side dish is an ideal accompaniment
to any roasted fowl.

Preparation Time: 20 minutes
Cooking Time: 12 to 14 minutes

INGREDIENTS

4	OZ/125 G CONCHIGLIE, CAVATELLI, *OR* OTHER DRIED SHAPED PASTA
1	OZ/30 G PANCETTA *OR* BACON, FINELY CHOPPED
1-1/2	OZ/45 G THINLY SLICED SPRING ONIONS
2	TABLESPOONS MARGARINE *OR* BUTTER
5	OZ/155 G FROZEN SMALL PEAS
1	TABLESPOON WATER
4	OZ/125 G MASCARPONE CHEESE
	SALT AND PEPPER (OPTIONAL)
1	TO 2 TABLESPOONS MILK (OPTIONAL)

67

*M*ascarpone is a buttery, rich and
delicately flavoured soft cheese from Italy.
*A suitable substitute is 4 oz/125 g of cream cheese
blended with 1 tablespoon of margarine or butter.*

■ In a large saucepan or pasta pot bring 3 qt/3 l water to boiling.
Add pasta. Reduce heat slightly. Boil, uncovered, for 12 to 14 minutes, or till
al dente, stirring occasionally. (Or, cook according to package directions.)
Drain immediately.

■ Meanwhile, in a medium saucepan cook and stir pancetta (if using) and onions in hot
margarine or butter for 2 minutes, or till onion is tender, but not brown. (If using bacon,
omit margarine or butter and cook with onions as directed.) Add frozen peas and water
to saucepan. Cover and simmer for 3 minutes. Gently stir in mascarpone cheese till
melted. If desired, season to taste with salt and pepper. Add hot cooked pasta and toss to
coat with cheese mixture. If mixture is too thick, add milk to thin to desired consistency.
Serve immediately.

Serves 6 as an accompaniment or entrée

Per serving: 178 calories, 6 g protein, 19 g carbohydrate, 9 g total fat (5 g saturated), 24 mg cholesterol, 88 mg sodium,
76 mg potassium

STEPS AT A GLANCE	Page
COOKING PASTA	12

Orecchiette with Fennel in Parmesan Cream

*T*ranslated from the Italian, orecchiette *means "little ears," a good description of their appearance. This is a very appealing pasta that can be made by hand (see page 53) or purchased dried. Here it combines with a complex sauce that features exotic mushrooms and strips of Italian ham.*

■ In a large saucepan or pasta pot bring 3 qt/3 l water to boiling. Add pasta. Reduce heat slightly. Boil, uncovered, 9 to 12 minutes for dried pasta or 2 to 3 minutes for fresh, or till al dente, stirring occasionally. (Or, cook according to package directions.) Drain.

■ Meanwhile, clean, trim, and slice the fennel bulb. Clean mushrooms; remove stems and discard. Slice mushroom caps.

■ In a large frying pan cook and stir the fennel over medium-high heat in hot margarine or butter for 3 minutes. Add the mushrooms and onion. Cook and stir for 5 minutes more. Add prosciutto and parsley.

■ In a small mixing bowl combine cream, Parmesan cheese, chicken stock, egg, anise liqueur or anise essence, and aniseed. Pour cream mixture into frying pan. Cook and stir till cheese melts and sauce thickens slightly. Add hot cooked pasta and toss to coat pasta well. Serve.

Serves 6 as an accompaniment or entrée

Per serving: 298 calories, 11 g protein, 20 g carbohydrate, 19 g total fat (8 g saturated), 69 mg cholesterol, 450 mg sodium, 212 mg potassium

Preparation Time: 20 minutes
Cooking Time: 10 minutes

INGREDIENTS

4	OZ/125 G DRIED *OR* 8 OZ/250 G FRESH ORECCHIETTE
1	FENNEL BULB
3	TO 4 OZ/90 TO 125 G FRESH SHIITAKE MUSHROOMS
3	TABLESPOONS MARGARINE *OR* BUTTER
2-1/2	OZ/75 G FINELY CHOPPED ONION
2	OZ/60 G PROSCIUTTO, CUT INTO THIN BITE-SIZE STRIPS
3/4	OZ/20 G CHOPPED FRESH PARSLEY
4	FL OZ/125 ML HEAVY (DOUBLE) CREAM
2	OZ/60 G GRATED PARMESAN CHEESE
2	FL OZ/60 ML CHICKEN STOCK
1	BEATEN EGG
1	TABLESPOON SAMBUCA OR OTHER ANISE LIQUEUR *OR* 1/2 TEASPOON ANISE ESSENCE
1/2	TEASPOON ANISEED

Anise liqueur and aniseed add an unexpected note of licorice to a sophisticated combination of vegetables and prosciutto.

Broccoli, Sausage & Shells in Balsamic Sauce

Lovers of spicy food will relish the fiery
jolt provided by hot Italian sausage
and crushed dried chili.

Preparation Time: 20 minutes
Cooking Time: 22 to 23 minutes

INGREDIENTS

6	OZ/185 G CONCHIGLIE, CAVATELLI, OR OTHER DRIED SHELL-SHAPED PASTA
8	OZ/250 G BROCCOLI FLORETS
12	OZ/375 G HOT ITALIAN-STYLE SAUSAGES
1	TABLESPOON OLIVE OIL OR COOKING OIL
2	CLOVES GARLIC, PEELED
1	TABLESPOON PLAIN FLOUR
1/8	TO 1/4 TEASPOON CRUSHED RED PEPPER (CHILI) FLAKES
8	FL OZ/250 ML CHICKEN STOCK
2	TABLESPOONS BALSAMIC VINEGAR

69

*I*talian balsamic vinegar is aged for years
in wooden barrels to mellow and sweeten.
Look for this unique condiment in gourmet food
shops and well-stocked supermarkets.

■ In a large saucepan or pasta pot bring 3 qt/3 l water to
boiling. Add pasta. Reduce heat slightly. Boil, uncovered, for
12 to 14 minutes, or till pasta is al dente, stirring occasionally.
Add broccoli to the pan during the last 5 minutes of cooking. (Or,
cook according to package directions, adding broccoli for the last 5
minutes.) Drain. Return pasta and broccoli to warm pan.

■ Meanwhile, in a large frying pan cook sausages, covered, in 4 fl oz/125 ml boiling water
for 15 minutes. Drain off liquid. Add olive oil and garlic to sausages in pan and cook, uncovered, for 4 to 5 minutes, turning sausages to brown them on all sides. Remove from
heat. Discard garlic and reserve 1 tablespoon of the pan drippings in the pan. Cool sausages,
then bias-slice into ¼-in/6-mm-thick pieces.

■ Stir flour and crushed red pepper into reserved drippings in pan. Add chicken stock all at
once. Cook and stir over medium heat till thickened and bubbly. Cook and stir for 2 minutes
more. Stir in balsamic vinegar. Pour chicken stock mixture over pasta-broccoli mixture. Add
sausages and toss to mix well; heat through. Serve immediately.

Serves 4 as a main course

Per serving: 460 calories, 23 g protein, 45 g carbohydrate, 21 g total fat (6 g saturated), 49 mg cholesterol, 804 mg sodium,
629 mg potassium

STEPS AT A GLANCE	Page
CUTTING FLORETS	36
COOKING PASTA	12

Rigatoni with Sausage & Mushroom Sauce

INGREDIENTS

1	LB/500 G ITALIAN-STYLE SAUSAGE MEAT (CASINGS REMOVED)
3	OZ/90 G SLICED FRESH MUSHROOMS
2	OZ/60 G CHOPPED ONION
15	OZ/425 G TINNED OR BOTTLED ITALIAN-STYLE TOMATO SAUCE
4	FL OZ/125 ML DRY WHITE OR RED WINE
2	TABLESPOONS CHOPPED PARSLEY
1	TEASPOON DRIED ITALIAN SEASONING, CRUSHED
1/2	TEASPOON SALT
1/4	TEASPOON PEPPER
8	OZ/250 G RIGATONI OR PENNE

Preparation Time: 15 minutes
Cooking Time: 45 to 50 minutes

STEPS AT A GLANCE	Page
PREPARING SAUCE INGREDIENTS	16
BROWNING MEAT	21
SIMMERING SAUCE	18
COOKING PASTA	12

*R*ib-sticking and chunky, this is an ideal cold-weather meal, perfect for serving after winter sports. Serve with a glass of red wine.

■ In a large frying pan cook sausage, mushrooms, and onion for 5 minutes, or till sausage is brown and onion and mushrooms are tender. Drain off fat. Add the tomato sauce, wine, parsley, Italian seasoning, salt, and pepper. Bring to boiling; reduce heat. Cover and simmer for 30 minutes. Uncover and simmer for 10 to 15 minutes more, or to desired consistency, stirring occasionally.

■ Meanwhile, in a large saucepan or pasta pot bring 3 qt/3 l water to boiling. Add pasta. Reduce heat slightly. Boil, uncovered, for 14 to 15 minutes, or till al dente, stirring occasionally. (Or, cook according to package directions.) Drain, then pour sauce over hot cooked pasta and serve.

Serves 4 as a main course

Per serving: 566 calories, 27 g protein, 57 g carbohydrate, 23 g total fat (8 g saturated), 66 mg cholesterol, 1,713 mg sodium, 822 mg potassium

Not fancy, but eminently satisfying: sausage, mushrooms, wine, and onions bound together in a hearty tomato sauce.

Baked Pasta & Cheddar with Ham

With the addition of chopped ham and vegetables, baked macaroni and cheese expands to a full-course meal that will satisfy everyone, young and old.

Preparation Time: 30 minutes
Baking Time: 30 minutes

INGREDIENTS

8	OZ/250 G TRICOLOURED OR PLAIN ROTINI OR OTHER DRIED SHAPED PASTA
1	MEDIUM CARROT, CUT INTO THIN, BITE-SIZE STRIPS
1	OZ/30 G CHOPPED ONION
2	OZ/60 G MARGARINE OR BUTTER
1-1/2	OZ/45 G PLAIN FLOUR
1/4	TEASPOON PEPPER
24	FL OZ/750 ML MILK
5	OZ/155 G SHREDDED CHEDDAR CHEESE
2-1/2	OZ/75 G CHOPPED GREEN PEPPER (CAPSICUM)
2-1/2	OZ/75 G CHOPPED RED PEPPER (CAPSICUM)
12	OZ/375 G CHOPPED COOKED HAM
1	OZ/30 G SHREDDED CHEDDAR CHEESE
	PEPPER (OPTIONAL)

71

*C*hopped carrots and peppers add a festive sprinkling of colour to this cheerful and easy casserole. It's a meal in itself served with steamed vegetables.

■ In a large saucepan or pasta pot bring 3 qt/3 l water to boiling. Add pasta. Reduce heat slightly. Boil, uncovered, for 8 to 10 minutes, or till pasta is al dente, stirring occasionally. Add carrot to boiling pasta the last 2 minutes of cooking. (Or, cook according to package directions, adding carrot the last 2 minutes.) Drain immediately.

■ Meanwhile, in a large saucepan cook onion in margarine or butter for 5 minutes, or till tender but not brown. Stir in flour and pepper. Add milk all at once. Cook and stir till slightly thickened and bubbly. Add 5 oz/155 g Cheddar cheese; stir till melted. Stir in pasta-carrot mixture, green and red pepper, and ham.

■ Transfer mixture to a 2-qt/2-l round casserole. Bake, covered, in a preheated 350°F/175°C oven for 25 minutes. Remove from oven and sprinkle with 1 oz/30 g Cheddar cheese and pepper, if desired. Return to oven and bake, uncovered, for 5 minutes more.

Serves 6 as a main course

Per serving: 476 calories, 26 g protein, 44 g carbohydrate, 21 g total fat (9 g saturated), 48 mg cholesterol, 933 mg sodium, 495 mg potassium

STEPS AT A GLANCE	Page
COOKING PASTA	12

Neapolitan Sauce with Penne

Unmistakably Italian, this sauce contains capers, anchovies, ripe olives, and other Mediterranean flavours.

Preparation Time: 15 minutes
Cooking Time: 20 minutes

INGREDIENTS

1-1/2	OZ/45 G FINELY CHOPPED ONION
2	CLOVES GARLIC, MINCED
1	TABLESPOON OLIVE OIL *OR* COOKING OIL
28	OZ/875 G TINNED WHOLE ITALIAN-STYLE TOMATOES, CUT UP
2	TABLESPOONS CHOPPED FRESH OREGANO *OR* 2 TEASPOONS DRIED OREGANO, CRUSHED
2	TABLESPOONS TOMATO PASTE
1	TABLESPOON CAPERS, DRAINED AND RINSED
1	TEASPOON SUGAR
1	TEASPOON ANCHOVY PASTE
1/8	TO 1/4 TEASPOON GROUND RED PEPPER (CAYENNE)
6	OZ/185 G PENNE, RIGATONI, *OR* OTHER DRIED SHAPED PASTA
1-1/2	OZ/45 G KALAMATA OLIVES, PITTED AND CHOPPED, *OR* PITTED BLACK OLIVES, CHOPPED
2	TABLESPOONS CHOPPED FRESH PARSLEY

A tiny dash of anchovy paste helps give the sauce for this pasta dish the inimitable flavour of Southern Italian cooking.

STEPS AT A GLANCE	Page
PREPARING SAUCE INGREDIENTS	16
SIMMERING SAUCE	18
COOKING PASTA	12

■ In a large saucepan cook the onion and garlic in hot oil till onion is tender but not brown. Stir in the undrained tomatoes, oregano, tomato paste, capers, sugar, anchovy paste, and red pepper. Bring to boiling; reduce heat. Simmer, uncovered, for about 20 minutes, or to desired consistency.

■ Meanwhile, in a large saucepan or pasta pot bring 3 qt/3 l water to boiling. Add pasta. Reduce heat slightly. Boil, uncovered, 14 to 15 minutes, or till al dente, stirring occasionally. (Or, cook according to package directions.) Drain immediately. Return pasta to warm pan.

■ Pour tomato mixture and olives over hot cooked pasta and toss to coat pasta. Transfer to a warm serving dish. Sprinkle with parsley and serve immediately.

Serves 6 as an accompaniment or entrée

Per serving: 179 calories, 6 g protein, 31 g carbohydrate, 4 g total fat (1 g saturated), 1 mg cholesterol, 304 mg sodium, 414 mg potassium

Broccoli & Pasta in Garlic Butter

Preparation Time: 15 minutes
Cooking Time: 12 to 14 minutes

INGREDIENTS

4	OZ/125 G RUOTE, CONCHIGLIE OR OTHER DRIED SHAPED PASTA
4	OZ/125 G BROCCOLI OR CAULIFLOWER FLORETS
1	TABLESPOON CHOPPED FRESH BASIL OR 1/2 TEASPOON DRIED BASIL, CRUSHED
2	CLOVES GARLIC, HALVED LENGTHWISE
2	TABLESPOONS MARGARINE OR BUTTER
2	TABLESPOONS OLIVE OIL OR COOKING OIL
1	OZ/30 G GRATED ROMANO OR PARMESAN CHEESE
	PEPPER (OPTIONAL)

*C*ombine crisp florets of broccoli or cauliflower with little pasta wheels *for an easy but delicious side dish that contrasts crisp and al dente textures. Another time, try the hybrid broccoflower, also known as broccolo Romano.*

■ In a large saucepan or pasta pot bring 3 qt/3 l water to boiling. Add pasta. Reduce heat slightly. Boil, uncovered, for 12 to 14 minutes, or till al dente, stirring occasionally. (Or, cook according to package directions.) Drain immediately.

■ Meanwhile, in a medium saucepan cook broccoli or cauliflower florets and basil, covered, in a small amount of boiling salted water for 6 to 8 minutes or till crisp-tender. Drain well. In a large frying pan cook the garlic in hot margarine or butter and olive oil or cooking oil for about 5 minutes, or till garlic is golden, stirring occasionally. Remove garlic from pan and discard.

■ Add broccoli or cauliflower florets to warm pan and toss to coat with margarine-oil mixture; heat through. Add hot cooked pasta and Romano or Parmesan cheese and toss to mix. Transfer to a warm serving dish. If desired, sprinkle with pepper. Serve immediately.

Serves 4 as an accompaniment or entrée

Per serving: 271 calories, 8 g protein, 27 g carbohydrate, 15 g total fat (3 g saturated), 7 mg cholesterol, 173 mg sodium, 269 mg potassium

73

A simple sauce of butter, olive oil, garlic, and broccoli is tossed with ruote (wagon-wheel pasta).

White Cheese & Macaroni

INGREDIENTS

4	OZ/125 G ELBOW MACARONI OR DITALINI
1	LARGE CLOVE GARLIC, CUT LENGTHWISE INTO SLIVERS
3	FL OZ/80 ML MILK
1	TABLESPOON MARGARINE OR BUTTER
4	OZ/125 G SHREDDED SHARP WHITE CHEDDAR CHEESE
1/4	TEASPOON WHITE OR BLACK PEPPER
1	TABLESPOON CHOPPED FRESH PARSLEY

Preparation Time: 15 minutes
Cooking Time: 10 to 13 minutes

STEPS AT A GLANCE	Page
COOKING PASTA	12

*T*he pasta can be cooked ahead, if you prefer. Drain, toss in a little oil, cover, and set aside for up to 2 hours or until needed. When preparing the sauce, return the cooked pasta to the saucepan, add the remaining ingredients, and finish the recipe as directed.

■ In a large saucepan or pasta pot bring 3 qt/3 l water to boiling. Add pasta and garlic slivers. Reduce heat slightly. Boil, uncovered, for 8 to 10 minutes, or till al dente, stirring occasionally. (Or, cook according to package directions.) Drain immediately.

■ Return pasta and garlic to warm pan. Add milk. Cook on low heat for 2 to 3 minutes, or till all the milk is absorbed by the pasta. Add margarine or butter, cheese, and pepper. Stir mixture gently till cheese is melted. Garnish with parsley and serve immediately.

Serves 4 as an accompaniment or entrée

Per serving: 275 calories, 12 g protein, 27 g carbohydrate, 13 g total fat (7 g saturated), 31 mg cholesterol, 221 mg sodium, 97 mg potassium

74

Sharp white Cheddar cheese and slivers of garlic transform a childhood favourite into a grown-up accompaniment for grilled fish or meat.

Layered Pasta

Steps in Making Layered Pasta

BAKING DISH

BASIC TOOLS FOR LAYERING PASTA

Equipment for preparing and serving layered pasta casseroles includes a chef's knife, assorted bowls, and spatulas. A pastry wheel and ruler are helpful when cutting fresh lasagne noodles.

CUTTING BOARD
AND GLASS BOWLS

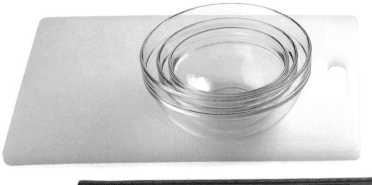

CHEF'S KNIFE

FLUTED PASTRY
WHEEL

RULER

METAL SPATULA

LARGE, WIDE SPATULA

76

L ASAGNE MADE WITH packaged noodles, cheese, and tomato-meat sauce is probably the most familiar layered pasta, but by no means the only one, as you will discover in this chapter. The steps and recipes that follow clearly demonstrate that layered pasta is a whole category of tempting recipes, not just a single dish.

The ingredients make the difference; the technique varies only slightly. Each is a construction of pasta and filling, with every layer contrasting yet complementing the others. Each is assembled in an ovenproof dish and baked until piping hot from top to bottom. All are hearty, satisfying, and good for casual party meals because they can be prepared in advance and reheated.

Lasagne Verdi, page 86, is a classic dish made with fresh or dried spinach noodles. Salmon Lasagne with Roasted Pepper Sauce, page 81, is a contemporary seafood casserole, and Vegetable Lasagne, page 84, dispenses with meat altogether to show off a cornucopia of vegetables. Three recipes use shaped pasta rather than flat sheets: Four Seasons Pasta Pie, page 78, has a spaghetti "crust," while both Greek-inspired Pastitsio, page 82, and Spicy Turkey & Corn Pasta, page 85, include macaroni.

dried pasta may
be substituted
for fresh pasta in
layered dishes

STEP 1 CUTTING FRESH LASAGNE NOODLES

Let the rolled fresh dough rest for about 20 minutes to dry slightly. Trim each piece to a large rectangle, as specified in the recipe. With a fluted pastry wheel or a sharp knife, cut each rectangle into even strips, using a ruler as a guide.

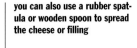

fresh noodles need only to be cooked briefly before layering

you can also use a rubber spatula or wooden spoon to spread the cheese or filling

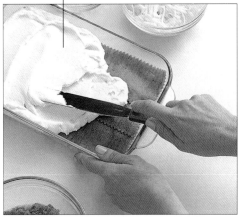

vary the recipe by using other kinds of shredded cheeses

STEP 2 SETTING THE NOODLES ASIDE

If necessary, trim the strips further to the size specified in the recipe. Place the strips on slightly damp kitchen towels so they won't dry out while you are cutting the remaining rectangles of dough. After cooking the noodles, place them on the towels to keep them from sticking together.

STEP 3 ASSEMBLING THE DISH

Cover the bottom of the dish with a little sauce to keep the noodles from sticking to the dish. Top with noodles, more sauce, and grated cheeses. Add the next layer of noodles. With a metal spatula, spread ricotta cheese or filling evenly across the noodles.

STEP 4 SPRINKLING WITH CHEESE

Arrange a layer of noodles over the filling. Spoon on the remaining sauce and spread to cover the pasta. Finish layering by sprinkling with the remaining cheeses.

77

the casserole will cut more easily if allowed to rest first to let the layers cool and set

Layers of fresh spinach pasta alternate with creamy cheeses and a rich meat sauce to make hearty Lasagne Verdi (page 86).

STEP 5 CUTTING INTO SERVINGS

Remove lasagne from the oven and let sit for 10 minutes. Cut into serving-size portions with a sharp knife. Transfer each portion to individual plates with a large, wide spatula.

Four Seasons Pasta Pie

Preparation Time: 30 minutes
Baking Time: 25 minutes

INGREDIENTS

CRUST

5	OZ/155 G DRIED SPAGHETTI *OR* LINGUINE *OR* 10 OZ/315 G FRESH LINGUINE
1	BEATEN EGG
1	OZ/30 G GRATED PARMESAN CHEESE
1	TABLESPOON MARGARINE *OR* BUTTER

CHEESE FILLING

1	BEATEN EGG
8	OZ/250 G RICOTTA CHEESE
1/8	TEASPOON PEPPER

TOPPING

1-1/2	OZ/45 G SLICED FRESH MUSHROOMS
1	TEASPOON OLIVE OIL
1	OZ/30 G PROSCIUTTO *OR* COOKED HAM, CHOPPED
2	PLUM (ROMA) TOMATOES, THINLY SLICED
4	TEASPOONS PESTO (PAGE 22)
2	TABLESPOONS GRATED PARMESAN CHEESE

78

If fresh plum tomatoes aren't in season, peel and thinly slice 1 large tomato, then cut the slices in half and arrange on top of the prosciutto or ham.

■ For crust, in a large saucepan or pasta pot bring 3 qt/3 l water to boiling. Add pasta. Reduce heat slightly. Boil, uncovered, 8 to 12 minutes for dried pasta or 1½ to 2 minutes for fresh, or till al dente, stirring occasionally. (Or, cook according to package directions.) Drain immediately. Return to warm pan.

■ Meanwhile, in a medium mixing bowl combine egg, Parmesan cheese, and margarine or butter. Pour over hot spaghetti in saucepan and toss to coat. Press spaghetti mixture evenly into bottom and up sides of a well-greased 9-in/23-cm pie plate.

■ For cheese filling, in a small mixing bowl combine egg, ricotta cheese, and pepper. Spread over spaghetti crust.

■ For topping, in a medium frying pan cook and stir mushrooms in hot oil for 2 minutes, or till tender. Set aside. Sprinkle chopped prosciutto or ham over cheese filling. Arrange tomato slices in a circle 1 in/2.5 cm from the edge of the pie plate. Dot pesto on tomato slices. Arrange mushrooms inside the circle of tomatoes.

■ Cover and bake in a preheated 350°F/180°C oven for 20 minutes. Uncover and sprinkle with Parmesan cheese. Bake, uncovered, for about 5 minutes more, or till cheese melts. Let stand for 5 to 10 minutes before serving. Cut into wedges to serve.

Serves 4 as a main course

Per serving: 513 calories, 27 g protein, 53 g carbohydrate, 21 g total fat (7 g saturated), 195 mg cholesterol, 495 mg sodium, 282 mg potassium

STEPS IN MAKING PASTA PIE

STEP 1 FORMING THE CRUST
With the back of a wooden spoon, press the spaghetti-egg mixture against the bottom and sides of a well-greased 9-in/23-cm pie plate.

STEP 2 DOTTING WITH PESTO
Spread the ricotta cheese mixture over the crust and top with the prosciutto or ham and tomatoes. Scoop up the pesto with a small spoon and push it off with a small spatula onto the tomatoes. Top with a ring of sautéed sliced mushrooms.

This savoury pie has a spaghetti "crust," a peppery cheese filling, and a topping of pesto, prosciutto or ham, mushrooms, and tomatoes.

Roasted peppers delicately tint and flavour the top layer of a seafood-and-pesto lasagne.

Salmon Lasagne with Roasted Pepper Sauce

Preparation Time: 1½ hours
Baking Time: 30 to 35 minutes

INGREDIENTS

12	OZ/375 G SKINLESS FRESH OR FROZEN SALMON FILLETS OR 12 OZ/375 G TINNED BONELESS, SKINLESS SALMON, DRAINED AND BROKEN UP
2	LARGE RED PEPPERS (CAPSICUMS)
3	FL OZ/80 ML PESTO (PAGE 22)
9	DRIED LASAGNE NOODLES
4	FL OZ/125 ML SOUR CREAM
1	TABLESPOON PLAIN FLOUR
1/4	TEASPOON SALT
1/8	TEASPOON PEPPER
1	BEATEN EGG
8	OZ/250 G RICOTTA CHEESE
8	OZ/250 G PACKAGED CREAM CHEESE, SOFTENED

*R*oasted red peppers have a completely different flavour from fresh ones. To use fresh lasagne noodles for this dish, follow the directions in the recipe on page 86, using 3 portions homemade pasta to make 9 noodles.

■ Thaw salmon, if frozen. Halve the red peppers; remove stems, seeds, and membranes. Place peppers, cut-side down, on a foil-lined baking sheet. Bake in a preheated 425°F/220°C oven for 20 to 25 minutes, or till skins are blistered and dark. Remove from baking sheet. Immediately place in a paper bag. Close bag; let stand about 30 minutes to steam the peppers so skins peel away more easily. (Or, place the bag in the freezer for 5 to 10 minutes.) Using a sharp knife, remove the skin from the peppers, pulling it off in strips. Discard skins. Reduce oven temperature to 375°F/190°C.

■ Meanwhile, prepare pesto as directed. Set aside. If using fresh or thawed frozen salmon fillets, in a large frying pan bring about 12 fl oz/375 ml water to boiling. Meanwhile, measure the thickness of the salmon fillets. Add salmon to pan. Return just to boiling and reduce heat. Cover and simmer for 4 to 6 minutes per ½-in/12-mm thickness. Drain, discarding cooking liquid. Use a fork to break fish into bite-size pieces. Set aside.

■ In a large saucepan or pasta pot bring 3 qt/3 l water to boiling. Add pasta. Reduce heat slightly. Boil, uncovered, for 10 to 12 minutes, or till al dente, stirring occasionally. (Or, cook according to package directions.) Drain immediately. Rinse with cold water; drain again.

■ In a food processor bowl or blender container, process or blend the roasted peppers till nearly smooth. Add sour cream, flour, salt, and pepper. Process or blend till combined. Set aside.

■ In a medium mixing bowl combine egg, ricotta cheese, and cream cheese. Stir in pesto and cooked or tinned salmon.

■ To assemble, lightly grease a 2-qt/2-l rectangular baking dish. Arrange 3 of the noodles in the bottom of the dish. Spread with one-third of the cheese mixture. Repeat layers twice. Carefully spread roasted red pepper mixture over the top layer.

■ Bake, uncovered, in a 375°F/190°C oven for 30 to 35 minutes, or till heated through. Let stand for 10 minutes before serving.

Serves 8 as a main course

Per serving: 386 calories, 17 g protein, 24 g carbohydrate, 25 g total fat (10 g saturated), 83 mg cholesterol, 309 mg sodium, 209 mg potassium

STEPS IN ROASTING PEPPERS AND POACHING SALMON

STEP 1 ROASTING PEPPERS

Place stemmed and seeded pepper halves on a foil-lined baking sheet. Roast in a preheated 425°F/220°C oven until the skins are blistered.

STEP 2 PEELING PEPPERS

After cooling the peppers, peel away the skin by pulling it off in strips with a sharp paring knife.

STEP 3 POACHING SALMON

Cook salmon in barely simmering water for 4 to 6 minutes per ½-in/12-mm thickness of fish. When done, lift out carefully with a wide spatula.

Pastitsio

STEPS AT A GLANCE	Page
PREPARING SAUCE INGREDIENTS	16
COOKING PASTA	12
LAYERING PASTITSIO	82

Preparation Time: 45 minutes (includes sauce)
Baking Time: 30 to 35 minutes

INGREDIENTS

MEAT SAUCE (PAGE 47)

PASTA

8	OZ/250 G ELBOW MACARONI
1	BEATEN EGG
1	OZ/30 G GRATED PARMESAN CHEESE

WHITE SAUCE

3	TABLESPOONS MARGARINE *OR* BUTTER
3	TABLESPOONS PLAIN FLOUR
1/4	TEASPOON PEPPER
12	FL OZ/375 ML MILK
1	BEATEN EGG
1	OZ/30 G GRATED PARMESAN CHEESE
	GROUND CINNAMON (OPTIONAL)

82

*T*he white sauce firms up into a creamy, delicious layer, and the cinnamon adds an exotic flavour to this traditional Greek dish.

■ Prepare the meat sauce as directed. Set aside.

■ For pasta, in a large saucepan or pasta pot bring 3 qt/3 l water to boiling. Add pasta. Reduce heat slightly. Boil, uncovered, for about 10 minutes, or till al dente, stirring occasionally. (Or, cook according to package directions.) Drain immediately. Rinse with cold water. Drain again.

■ In a large mixing bowl combine 1 beaten egg, 1 oz/30 g Parmesan cheese, and hot cooked macaroni. Set aside.

■ For white sauce, in a medium saucepan melt margarine or butter. Stir in flour and pepper. Add the milk all at once. Cook and stir till thickened and bubbly. Stir about half the mixture into 1 beaten egg. Return egg mixture to the saucepan. Stir in 1 oz/30 g Parmesan cheese.

■ To assemble, layer half of the pasta mixture in a greased 2-qt/2-l square baking dish. Top with all the meat sauce, the remaining pasta mixture, and all the white sauce. If desired, sprinkle lightly with cinnamon.

■ Bake in a preheated 350°F/180°C oven for 30 to 35 minutes, or till set. Let stand for 5 minutes before serving.

Serves 6 as a main course

Per serving: 429 calories, 26 g protein, 45 g carbohydrate, 16 g total fat (5 g saturated), 118 mg cholesterol, 672 mg sodium, 660 mg potassium

STEPS IN LAYERING PASTITSIO

STEP 1 MAKING PASTA MIXTURE

Cook the macaroni, then drain thoroughly. In a large mixing bowl, combine the pasta with the egg and grated Parmesan cheese. Mix well.

STEP 2 LAYERING

Spread half the pasta mixture on the bottom of a 2-qt/2-l baking dish. Cover with the meat sauce. Then, spoon on the remaining pasta so that it covers the sauce completely. Top with all the white sauce.

A simple vegetable accompaniment
such as grilled eggplant (aubergine)
and fresh tomato will go nicely with
this traditional Greek pasta casserole.

Vegetable Lasagne

To prepare this dish with fresh lasagne noodles, follow the directions in the recipe on page 86, using 2 portions of homemade pasta. If you want to use fresh artichoke hearts, prepare them as directed on page 59, then blanch them for about 5 minutes.

- In a large saucepan or pasta pot bring 3 qt/3 l water to boiling. Add pasta. Reduce heat slightly. Boil, uncovered, for 10 to 12 minutes, or till al dente, stirring occasionally. (Or, cook according to package directions.) Drain immediately. Rinse with cold water; drain again.

- For vegetables, cook artichoke hearts according to package directions. Drain and chop. In a large frying pan cook mushrooms and carrots in margarine or butter for 3 minutes, or till tender. Stir in chopped artichoke hearts. Set vegetable mixture aside.

- For sauce, in a medium saucepan cook spring onion and garlic in hot margarine or butter till tender. Stir in flour and pepper. Add light cream or milk and chicken stock all at once. Cook and stir till thickened and bubbly. Remove from heat and set aside. For filling, in a medium mixing bowl combine spinach, cottage cheese, and Parmesan cheese; set aside.

- To assemble, grease a 2-qt/2-l rectangular baking dish. Arrange 3 noodles in the prepared dish. Spread half of the filling on top of the noodles. Spoon half the vegetable mixture over the filling. Spoon half the sauce over top. Repeat layers.

- Bake, covered, in a preheated 350°F/180°C oven for 35 minutes. Uncover and sprinkle 1 oz/30 g Parmesan cheese over the top. Bake for 5 to 10 minutes more, or till mixture is heated through. Let stand for 10 minutes before serving.

Serves 8 as a main course

Per serving: 233 calories, 13 g protein, 26 g carbohydrate, 10 g total fat (4 g saturated), 18 mg cholesterol, 415 mg sodium, 471 mg potassium

84

STEPS AT A GLANCE	Page
COOKING PASTA	12
PREPARING SAUCE INGREDIENTS	16
MAKING LAYERED PASTA	76

Preparation Time: 40 minutes
Baking Time: 40 to 45 minutes

INGREDIENTS

6	DRIED LASAGNE NOODLES

VEGETABLES

9	OZ/280 G PACKAGE FROZEN ARTICHOKE HEARTS
8	OZ/250 G SLICED FRESH MUSHROOMS
5	OZ/155 G SHREDDED CARROTS
1	TABLESPOON MARGARINE *OR* BUTTER

SAUCE

1-1/2	OZ/45 G SLICED SPRING ONIONS
2	CLOVES GARLIC, MINCED
1	TABLESPOON MARGARINE *OR* BUTTER
1	OZ/30 G PLAIN FLOUR
1/4	TEASPOON PEPPER
8	FL OZ/250 ML LIGHT (SINGLE) CREAM *OR* MILK
6	FL OZ/185 ML CHICKEN STOCK

FILLING

10	OZ/315 G FROZEN CHOPPED SPINACH, THAWED AND DRAINED
8	OZ/250 G CREAM-STYLE COTTAGE CHEESE, DRAINED
1	OZ/30 G GRATED PARMESAN CHEESE

TOPPING

1	OZ/30 G GRATED PARMESAN CHEESE

Chunky vegetables such as artichoke hearts, mushrooms, and carrots add appealing texture and crunch to a meatless lasagne.

Spicy Turkey & Corn Pasta

Preparation Time: 30 minutes
Baking Time: 30 to 45 minutes

INGREDIENTS

12	OZ/375 G MINCED UNCOOKED TURKEY MEAT
2	OZ/60 G CHOPPED ONION
1	CLOVE GARLIC, MINCED
15	OZ/425 G TINNED *OR* BOTTLED ITALIAN-STYLE TOMATO SAUCE
8	FL OZ/250 ML WATER
2	TABLESPOONS CHOPPED FRESH CORIANDER LEAVES (OPTIONAL)
1	TABLESPOON TOMATO PASTE
1/2	TEASPOON SALT
1/2	TEASPOON GROUND CUMIN
1/4	TEASPOON CHILI POWDER
1/4	TEASPOON GROUND CORIANDER
1/8	TEASPOON GROUND RED PEPPER (CAYENNE)
4	OZ/125 G CORN *OR* PLAIN ELBOW MACARONI
8	OZ/250 G TINNED RED KIDNEY BEANS, DRAINED
4	OZ/125 G SHREDDED PROVOLONE CHEESE

85

*I*f you like Mexican food, here's a one-course meal chock-full of all your favourite Mexican spices. Look for the corn elbow macaroni at health food shops; it is often used by people on wheat-free diets.

A fruit garnish of juicy orange wedges and tart-sweet kiwifruit helps to cool the fire of a spicy Mexican pasta main course.

■ In a large frying pan cook the turkey, onion, and garlic for 5 minutes, or till meat is brown. Drain off fat. Add tomato sauce, water, coriander leaves (if desired), tomato paste, salt, cumin, chili powder, ground coriander, and red pepper. Bring to boiling; reduce heat. Cover and simmer for 15 minutes.

■ Lightly grease a 2-qt/2-l square baking dish. Layer half the uncooked elbow macaroni, half the turkey mixture, half the beans, and half the cheese. Repeat layers.

■ Bake, covered, in a preheated 350°F/180°C oven for 20 minutes (40 minutes for plain macaroni). Uncover and bake for 10 minutes more (5 minutes more for plain macaroni), or till pasta is tender and mixture is heated through. Let stand for 10 minutes before serving.

Serves 6 as a main course

Per serving: 327 calories, 19 g protein, 26 g carbohydrate, 18 g total fat (4 g saturated), 17 mg cholesterol, 826 mg sodium, 403 mg potassium

STEPS AT A GLANCE	Page
PREPARING SAUCE INGREDIENTS	16
SIMMERING SAUCE	18
LAYERING	82

Lasagne Verdi

This appealing lasagne displays all the colours of the Italian flag: green spinach noodles, creamy white cheese, and tomato-red sauce.

Preparation Time: 1¼ hours (includes sauce)
Baking Time: 30 minutes

INGREDIENTS

9	DRIED SPINACH OR PLAIN LASAGNE NOODLES *OR* 3 PORTIONS HOMEMADE PASTA (PAGE 14)
	BOLOGNESE SAUCE (PAGE 21)
2	TABLESPOONS MARGARINE *OR* BUTTER
2	TABLESPOONS PLAIN FLOUR
1/4	TEASPOON SALT
	DASH PEPPER
5	FL OZ/160 ML MILK
4	OZ/125 G RICOTTA CHEESE
8	OZ/250 G SHREDDED MOZZARELLA CHEESE
1	OZ/30 G GRATED PARMESAN CHEESE

*I*n Italian, verdi *means "green," and green spinach pasta is what gives this recipe its name. You can use plain pasta if you prefer.*

■ If using homemade pasta, roll each portion of dough to a 12x9-in/30x23-cm rectangle. Cut into three 12x2½-in/30x6-cm noodles.

■ Prepare Bolognese sauce, except omit the cream and nutmeg. Set aside. In a small saucepan melt margarine or butter. Stir in flour, salt, and pepper. Add milk all at once. Cook and stir over medium heat till thickened and bubbly. Stir in ricotta cheese.

■ In a large saucepan or pasta pot bring 3 qt/3 l water to boiling. Add pasta. Reduce heat slightly. Boil, uncovered, for 10 to 12 minutes for dried pasta or 2 to 3 minutes for fresh, or till al dente, stirring occasionally. (Or, cook according to package directions.) Drain immediately. Rinse with cold water; drain again.

■ Spread 4 fl oz/125 ml of the Bolognese sauce in the bottom of a greased 2-qt/2-l rectangular baking dish. Arrange one-third of the noodles on top of the sauce. Spread with half the remaining Bolognese sauce. Sprinkle with half the mozzarella and half the Parmesan. Add another layer of noodles and all the ricotta mixture. Repeat layers with remaining noodles, Bolognese sauce, mozzarella, and Parmesan. Bake, uncovered, in a preheated 375°F/190°C oven for 30 minutes, or till heated through. Let stand for 10 minutes before serving.

Serves 6 to 8 as a main course

Per serving: 534 calories, 33 g protein, 47 g carbohydrate, 23 g total fat (10 g saturated), 70 mg cholesterol, 732 mg sodium, 878 mg potassium

Stuffed Pasta

Steps in Stuffing Pasta

SMALL AND MEDIUM BOWLS

ROLLING PIN

RAVIOLI FRAME

SOFT PAINTBRUSH

MEASURING TEASPOON

CUTTING BOARD

FLUTED PASTRY WHEEL

BASIC TOOLS FOR MAKING STUFFED PASTA

A ravioli frame allows for assembly-line efficiency when filling, sealing, and scoring pasta squares, but it is almost as easy to shape them by hand and cut them with a pastry wheel. Bowls and a measuring spoon are also necessary for stuffing pasta, and a small paintbrush is helpful for sealing.

88

ALTHOUGH DELICATE AND TENDER, fresh pasta is sturdy enough to serve as edible wrapping for all sorts of tasty bundles. Some enclose the filling completely so that the first bite is a delicious surprise. These include square ravioli, half-moon-shaped agnolotti, and ring-shaped tortellini. Tubular cannelloni and manicotti — discussed on page 90 — and their close kin the pasta roll (see Stuffed Pasta Rolls, page 92) are left partially open to reveal some of the savoury mixture encased within.

Classic fillings incorporate cheeses like creamy ricotta and pungent grated Parmesan, and chopped spinach or ham, all bound with a little egg. Others feature meaty mushrooms, spicy sausage seasoned with herbs, or intensely tasty dried tomatoes. These pastas and fillings nicely mix and match, so you can experiment and interchange them for variety.

Regardless of their final form, all these packages begin with a basic pasta dough rolled by hand or with a machine into thin sheets as for lasagne or ribbon pasta. To review this technique, see Steps for Making Pasta, pages 8 to 11. Unlike ribbon pasta, however, pasta for stuffing must be pliable. Don't let the rolled sheet dry

or you won't be able to shape it. Use immediately and cover unused portions with a kitchen towel or plastic wrap until needed.

Shape and fill ravioli and tortellini one step at a time. Always leave a sufficient margin of dough around the filling to ensure a good seal. For a different look, vary the size by using large, wide strips for ravioli or bigger circles for tortellini. A trio or quartet of 3-in/7.5-cm ravioli looks quite dramatic as a first course. Create an attractive edge on either ravioli or tortellini by cutting with a fluted pastry wheel or scalloped cutter.

Forming ravioli by hand is very easy, but a metal frame already moulded with indentations and scoring notches will speed the process up. Most kitchenware shops or larger store kitchenware departments stock these. Both hand and frame methods for ravioli are shown in steps 1 to 4 at right.

Stuffed pasta can be made early in the day and cooked close to serving time. Arrange on a flour-dusted tray, lightly dust with flour, and refrigerate, covered with a kitchen towel. Don't let the pieces touch or they might stick together and tear when you try to separate them.

press out as much air as
possible around filling
before sealing

press down the edges
of the cut ravioli one
more time to seal

one teaspoonful is
about the proper
amount of filling

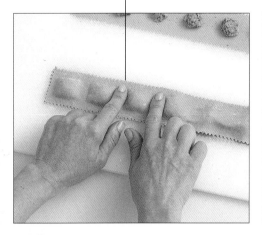

STEP 1 SEALING RAVIOLI

On each 2x12-in/5x30-cm strip of dough, arrange 1 teaspoon of filling every 2 in/5 cm, beginning 1 in/2.5 cm from one end. Moisten the dough around the filling with a small paintbrush or your finger, top with another strip of dough and press down on either side of the filling to seal.

STEP 2 CUTTING RAVIOLI

With a fluted pastry cutter or sharp knife, cut halfway between the mounds of filling to separate the ravioli. Repeat with the remaining pasta and filling.

STEP 3 MAKING RAVIOLI WITH A FRAME

Drape a sheet of fresh dough on the bottom of the frame. Press lightly into each hollow, or set the top of the frame (if there is one) on the dough and press gently. Place about 1 teaspoon of filling in each hollow.

89

after sealing, remove the
ravioli from the frame and
pull them apart at the seams

you can work faster
if you fill a number of
circles at one time

if the dough has dried out,
moisten the ends before
you pinch them together

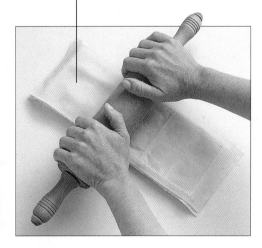

STEP 4 SEALING RAVIOLI IN A FRAME

Brush the dough lightly with water. Set another rectangle of dough on top of the filling. Using firm, even pressure, push a wooden rolling pin across. Or, apply the top of the frame, if there is one. This action both seals the ravioli and scores them.

STEP 5 FOLDING TORTELLINI

Stamp out little rounds of dough with a 1½-in/4-cm round cutter. Place about ¼ teaspoon filling in the centre of each round. Brush the edge with water. Create a half-moon by folding the dough circle in half. Pinch along the edge to seal.

STEP 6 SHAPING TORTELLINI

Bend the half-moon, seam-side out, and bring the two outer ends together. Pinch them to seal. For larger tortellini, shape by placing a finger against the fold and bending around it; overlap the ends and pinch.

Steps in Stuffing Manicotti and Cannelloni

BASIC TOOLS FOR MANICOTTI AND CANNELLONI

A ruler and rolling cutter make quick work of dividing pasta sheets into uniform squares or rectangles. Use a small spoon to fill cooked tubes so that their delicate walls won't tear. An oven-proof baking dish holds the finished product.

CUTTING BOARD AND BAKING DISH

BOWL

PIZZA CUTTER

SPOON

RULER

90

Manicotti and cannelloni are luscious rolls of pasta wrapped around cheese, meat, and vegetables. Both are easily assembled using paper-thin squares or rectangles of fresh dough or dried pasta tubes. The two are essentially the same dish with one difference: Manicotti are rolled on the diagonal, while cannelloni are rolled straight across. As seems to be true with all Italian pasta, even such a slight variation is inspiration for an entirely new name.

Both fresh pasta squares or rectangles and dried pasta tubes must be cooked in boiling water until just al dente. Don't overcook or overstuff dried pasta tubes, or they will burst as they expand during baking. For a more attractive shape, always roll cooked fresh pasta in a tight bundle around the filling.

Chicken-filled Classic Cannelloni, page 104, is topped with tomato and cheese sauces side by side. Grilled Spinach Cannelloni, page 103, is quickly browned under the grill and covered with a lemony cream sauce. Manicotti with Roasted Vegetables, page 102, is baked with fresh tomato sauce and a topping of garlic-infused vegetables.

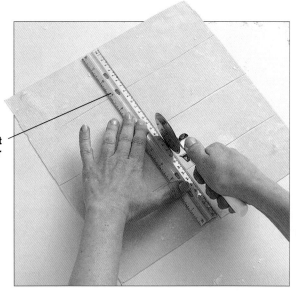

to make straight cuts, use a ruler as a guide

STEP 1 CUTTING PASTA SHEETS

Roll pasta into a thin sheet. Cut the sheet of dough into squares or rectangles, as directed in the recipe. Use a pizza cutter, a fluted pastry wheel, or a sharp knife.

use gentle pressure when rolling so the filling isn't squeezed out

fill from the centre to the open end, then turn and fill the other end

some of the filling will be exposed at either end

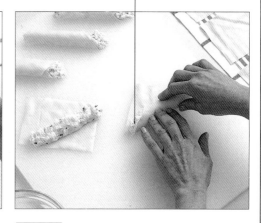

STEP 2 FILLING CANNELLONI

Cook the pasta squares or rectangles until al dente. Drain and place on a kitchen towel. Spoon the filling along one edge of each cooked pasta piece. Roll the dough tightly around the filling.

STEP 3 FILLING DRIED MANICOTTI

Cook the shells until al dente. Drain and place on a kitchen towel. With a small spoon, carefully insert equal amounts of filling into each shell; do not pack filling.

STEP 4 FILLING FRESH MANICOTTI

Cook the pasta rectangles until al dente. Drain and place on a kitchen towel. Place rectangles with one corner toward you. Spoon equal amounts of filling diagonally across and just below the centre of each rectangle. Beginning at the bottom corner, roll the dough around the filling.

91

set them seam-side down so they won't unroll

STEP 5 PLACING IN BAKING DISH

Carefully transfer filled cannelloni or manicotti to a baking dish. Arrange rolled pasta in the dish with the seams on the bottom.

Roll cooked pasta squares or rectangles around the filling of your choice, top with a simple tomato sauce and bake.

Stuffed Pasta Rolls

Preparation Time: 1½ hours
Baking Time: 20 minutes

INGREDIENTS

1	PORTION (4 OZ/125 G) SPINACH PASTA (PAGE 14)

FILLING

1/2	OZ/15 G FRESH CHIVES
1/2	OZ/15 G FRESH PARSLEY
1	OR 2 SMALL CLOVES GARLIC
8	OZ/250 G PACKAGED CREAM CHEESE
4	OZ/125 G CREAM-STYLE COTTAGE CHEESE
5	OZ/155 G THINLY SLICED CAPICOLLO, PROSCIUTTO, OR HAM
4	OZ/125 G DRAINED AND FINELY CHOPPED OIL-PACKED DRIED TOMATOES

SAUCE

6	OZ/180 G SLICED FRESH MUSHROOMS
2	CLOVES GARLIC, MINCED
3	TABLESPOONS MARGARINE OR BUTTER
3	TABLESPOONS PLAIN FLOUR
1/4	TEASPOON SALT
1/4	TEASPOON WHITE PEPPER
8	FL OZ/250 ML CHICKEN STOCK
8	FL OZ/250 ML LIGHT (SINGLE) CREAM OR MILK
1/2	TEASPOON FINELY SHREDDED LEMON PEEL
1	TABLESPOON LEMON JUICE

*P*asta rolls are impressive to serve and surprisingly simple to make. When sliced, these reveal spirals of green pasta and a filling of ham, cheese, and chewy dried tomatoes. The rolls may be prepared 1 day ahead and refrigerated until ready to bake.

■ Prepare spinach pasta as directed, except divide the portion of dough in half and roll each half to a 12x6-in/30x15-cm rectangle. In a large saucepan or pasta pot bring 3 qt/3 l water to boiling. Add 1 sheet of the pasta. Reduce heat slightly. Boil, uncovered, about 3 minutes, or till pasta is al dente, stirring occasionally. Use a slotted spoon to carefully lift pasta from water and into a colander. Rinse with cold water. Drain well. Carefully spread on a damp cloth towel. Repeat with remaining pasta sheet.

■ Meanwhile, for filling, in a food processor bowl or blender container finely chop the chives, parsley, and garlic. Add cream cheese and cottage cheese and blend till nearly smooth.

■ To assemble, spread half the filling over each pasta sheet to within ¼ in/6 mm of the edges. Arrange the capicollo, prosciutto, or ham and chopped dried tomatoes in layers on top of the filling. Roll jam-roll style, starting from one of the short sides. (If desired, cover pasta roll tightly and chill for up to 24 hours.) Trim uneven edges of rolls. Cut each roll into 6 slices. Place the slices, cut-side down, in a 2-qt/2-l rectangular baking dish. Bake, covered, in a pre-heated 375°F/190°C oven for about 20 minutes, or till heated through.

■ Meanwhile, for sauce, in a medium saucepan cook mushrooms and garlic in hot margarine or butter till tender. Stir in flour, salt, and pepper. Add chicken stock and light cream or milk all at once. Cook and stir till thickened and bubbly. Cook and stir for 1 minute more. Remove from heat and stir in lemon peel and lemon juice. To serve, divide sauce among individual plates. Arrange hot pasta pinwheels on top of sauce. Serve immediately.

Serves 4 to 6 as a main course

Per serving: 520 calories, 25 g protein, 30 g carbohydrate, 34 g total fat (16 g saturated), 104 mg cholesterol, 1,303 mg sodium, 787 mg potassium

STEPS IN MAKING PASTA ROLLS

STEP 2 CUTTING PASTA

Trim away uneven ends of pasta rolls. Cut each roll into 6 slices with a serrated knife. Place the slices, cut-side down, in a baking dish. Cover with aluminium foil and bake as directed.

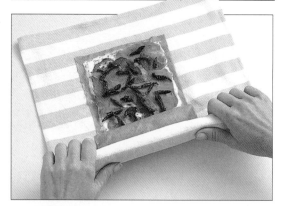

STEP 1 ROLLING PASTA

Begin at one short end. Roll pasta and filling jam-roll style by rolling up the towel to gently push the dough along.

Colourful pinwheels of spinach pasta and filling make a stunning presentation.

94

Crisp lumpia are filled with a mixture
of prawns and pork flavoured with spicy
fresh ginger. Serve as an hors d'oeuvre or
entrée with a garlicky dipping sauce.

Lumpia

INGREDIENTS

FILLING

2	OZ/60 G CHOPPED ONION
2	CLOVES GARLIC, MINCED
1	TEASPOON GRATED FRESH GINGER ROOT
1	TABLESPOON COOKING OIL
4	OZ/125 G FINELY CHOPPED PEELED AND DEVEINED PRAWNS
4	OZ/125 G FINELY CHOPPED COOKED PORK
2	FL OZ/60 ML WATER
2	TABLESPOONS SOY SAUCE
1/8	TEASPOON PEPPER

SAUCE

2	CLOVES GARLIC, MINCED
1	TEASPOON COOKING OIL
1	TEASPOON CORNFLOUR
4	FL OZ/125 ML VINEGAR
2	TABLESPOONS WATER

LUMPIA

12	LUMPIA WRAPPERS (FILIPINO PASTRY WRAPPERS) OR SPRING ROLL WRAPPERS
	COOKING OIL FOR FRYING

*F**ilipino-style egg rolls, or lumpia, are about 6 in/15 cm long and about as thick as a small cigar. Serve them as a delicious appetiser or entrée.*

■ For filling, in a large frying pan cook onion, garlic, and ginger root in hot oil for 5 minutes, or till tender, but not brown. Add prawns and cook till they turn pink, stirring constantly. Add cooked pork, water, soy sauce, and pepper. Cook till liquid is evaporated.

■ Meanwhile, for sauce, in a small frying pan or saucepan cook garlic in hot oil till tender. In a small mixing bowl combine cornflour, vinegar, and water. Carefully add to pan. Cook and stir till sauce is slightly thickened and bubbly. Cook and stir for 1 minute more. Set aside.

■ To assemble lumpia, place a lumpia or spring roll wrapper on a flat surface in front of you. Spoon 2 tablespoons of the filling nearly across the width of the wrapper. Roll the wrapper once to cover the filling, then fold sides towards centre. Moisten edges with water and continue to roll tightly.

■ In a large frying pan heat 1 in/2.5 cm of cooking oil to 365°F/185°C. Fry lumpia, a few at a time, for 2 to 3 minutes, or till golden brown. Drain on paper towels. Serve immediately with sauce.

Makes 12 rolls

Per serving: 190 calories, 12 g protein, 14 g carbohydrate, 10 g total fat (2 g saturated), 68 mg cholesterol, 372 mg sodium, 186 mg potassium

Preparation Time: 40 minutes
Cooking Time: 6 to 9 minutes

STEPS AT A GLANCE	Page
PREPARING SAUCE INGREDIENTS	16
PEELING PRAWNS	36
MAKING LUMPIA	95

95

STEPS IN MAKING LUMPIA

STEP 1 FILLING

Prepare the filling and place in a bowl nearby. Spoon 2 tablespoons of the filling across the width of each dough wrapper. Leave a slight margin of space at either end.

STEP 2 ROLLING

Roll the wrapper once to cover the filling, then fold the sides toward the centre. Moisten the edges with water and continue to roll tightly.

STEP 3 FRYING

Heat oil to proper temperature in a large frying pan. Drop a few lumpia at a time into the hot fat with a wide metal spatula. Cook until golden brown, remove, and drain.

Mushroom-filled Ravioli

Preparation Time: 1 hour
Cooking Time: 20 minutes

STEPS AT A GLANCE	Page
MAKING PASTA	8–14
STUFFING PASTA	88
PREPARING SAUCE INGREDIENTS	16

Ravioli with a filling of thyme-scented mushrooms: elegant fare for any special occasion.

96

A mixture of several types of mushrooms will add a deep, woody flavour to the ravioli filling. These make a beautiful first course, light supper, or hot hors d'oeuvre served in a chafing dish with toothpicks for spearing.

■ Prepare spinach pasta as directed, except roll each portion of dough into an 8x12-in/20x30-cm rectangle. Cover and set aside.

■ For filling, in a large frying pan cook mushrooms, onion, and garlic in hot margarine or butter for 5 minutes, or till tender. In a medium mixing bowl combine egg, bread crumbs, Parmesan cheese, and thyme. Stir in mushroom mixture. Set aside.

■ To make ravioli, cut each portion of pasta into four 2x12-in/5x30-cm strips. Brush one side of one strip with water. Place about 2 teaspoons of filling every 2 in/5 cm, beginning 1 in/2.5 cm from the end of one of the pieces. Take second strip and place it over the top of the filling. Press pasta together between the mounds of filling. Use a 2-in/5-cm ravioli cutter, square biscuit cutter, or sharp knife to cut between the ravioli. Press the edges down firmly again to seal. Repeat with remaining pasta and filling.

■ For sauce, in a small saucepan heat cream over medium heat for about 15 minutes, or till bubbly, stirring frequently. Boil gently for 3 to 4 minutes more.

■ Meanwhile, in a large saucepan or pasta pot bring 3 qt/3 l water to boiling. Add half of the pasta. Reduce heat slightly. Boil, uncovered, for 6 to 8 minutes, or till al dente, stirring occasionally. Remove pasta from boiling water with a slotted spoon and place in a greased casserole. Cover and keep warm in a preheated 300°F/150°C oven while cooking remaining pasta. Pour thickened cream over cooked ravioli. If desired, sprinkle with fresh thyme. Serve immediately.

Serves 6 as an entrée

Per serving: 262 calories, 7 g protein, 16 g carbohydrate, 20 g total fat (11 g saturated), 111 mg cholesterol, 301 mg sodium, 164 mg potassium

INGREDIENTS

2	PORTIONS (8 OZ/250 G) SPINACH PASTA (PAGE 14)

FILLING

4	OZ/125 G FINELY CHOPPED FRESH MUSHROOMS
1-1/2	OZ/45 G FINELY CHOPPED ONION
1	CLOVE GARLIC, MINCED
1	TABLESPOON MARGARINE *OR* BUTTER
1	BEATEN EGG
1	OZ/30 G SEASONED FINE BREAD CRUMBS
1	OZ/30 G GRATED PARMESAN CHEESE
1/4	TEASPOON DRIED THYME, CRUSHED

SAUCE

8	FL OZ/250 ML HEAVY (DOUBLE) CREAM
	FRESH THYME LEAVES (OPTIONAL)

Meat-stuffed Ravioli

INGREDIENTS

Preparation Time: 1 hour
Cooking Time: 12 to 16 minutes

2	PORTIONS (8 OZ/250 G) HOMEMADE PASTA (PAGE 14)
	CLASSIC TOMATO SAUCE (PAGE 18) *OR* 28 FL OZ/875 ML TINNED *OR* BOTTLED ITALIAN-STYLE TOMATO SAUCE
1	BEATEN EGG
1-1/2	OZ/45 G SOFT BREAD CRUMBS
2	TABLESPOONS DRY RED WINE
1	CLOVE GARLIC, MINCED
1	TEASPOON FENNEL SEED, CRUSHED
1/4	TEASPOON ITALIAN SEASONING, CRUSHED
1/4	TEASPOON SALT
1/8	TEASPOON PEPPER
12	OZ/375 G LEAN GROUND (MINCED) BEEF *OR* VEAL
1	OZ/30 G GRATED PARMESAN CHEESE

97

*U*sing egg roll wrappers is a good way to cut down on the preparation time for this recipe. Simply substitute 48 wrappers for the pasta and cook for 6 to 8 minutes.

■ Prepare fresh pasta as directed, except roll each portion of the dough into an 8x12-in/20x30-cm rectangle. Cover and set aside.

■ If using classic tomato sauce, prepare as directed. Set aside.

■ In a mixing bowl stir together egg, bread crumbs, wine, garlic, fennel seed, Italian seasoning, salt, and pepper. Add beef or veal and mix well. Shape meat mixture into a 6x4-in/15x10-cm rectangle. Cut into twenty-four 1-in/2.5-cm squares.

■ To make ravioli, cut each portion of pasta into four 2x12-in/5x30 cm strips. Brush one side of one strip with water. Place 1 meat square every 2 in/5 cm, beginning 1 in/2.5 cm from the end on one of the pieces. Take the second strip of pasta and place it over the top of the filling. Press pasta together between the meat squares. Use a 2-in/5-cm ravioli cutter, square biscuit cutter, or sharp knife to cut between the ravioli. Press the edges down firmly again to seal. Repeat with remaining pasta and filling.

■ Meanwhile, in a large saucepan or pasta pot bring 3 qt/3 l water to boiling. Add half of the ravioli. Reduce heat slightly. Boil, uncovered, for 6 to 8 minutes, or till meat in ravioli is no longer pink and pasta is al dente, stirring occasionally. Remove ravioli from boiling water with a slotted spoon and place in a greased casserole. Cover and keep warm in a preheated 300°F/150°C oven while cooking remaining ravioli. Serve tomato sauce over hot cooked ravioli. Sprinkle with Parmesan cheese and serve immediately.

Serves 4 as a main course

Per serving: 642 calories, 33 g protein, 77 g carbohydrate, 24 g total fat (6 g saturated), 165 mg cholesterol, 638 mg sodium, 1,576 mg potassium

With very little effort, you can make ravioli that compare to the best restaurant pasta. Serve with a simple tomato sauce, a salad, and garlic bread.

STEPS AT A GLANCE	Page
MAKING PASTA	8–14
STUFFING PASTA	88
PREPARING SAUCE INGREDIENTS	16
MAKING TOMATO SAUCE	18

Ham Tortellini with Cheese Sauce

Tiny stuffed tortellini are made
from little circles of spinach
pasta that are filled, sealed,
and folded in half.

Preparation Time: 1½ hours
Cooking Time: 12 to 16 minutes

INGREDIENTS

2	PORTIONS (8 OZ/250 G) SPINACH PASTA (PAGE 14)

FILLING

2	TABLESPOONS FINELY CHOPPED CELERY
2	TABLESPOONS FINELY CHOPPED ONION
2	TEASPOONS MARGARINE *OR* BUTTER
4	OZ/125 G GROUND (MINCED) COOKED HAM
1	BEATEN EGG YOLK

SAUCE

2	TABLESPOONS MARGARINE *OR* BUTTER
4	TEASPOONS PLAIN FLOUR
8	FL OZ/250 ML MILK
2	OZ/60 G SHREDDED SWISS CHEESE
2	TABLESPOONS CHOPPED FRESH PARSLEY

*H*ere's an unusual pasta using a popular combination:
ham and Swiss cheese. Spinach pasta adds colour and
extra flavour to the dish.

■ Prepare and roll spinach pasta as directed. With a 1½-in/4-cm round
cutter, cut 96 circles from dough. Cover and set aside.

■ For filling, cook celery and onion in hot margarine or butter till tender. Remove from heat
and stir in ham and egg yolk. Place about ¼ teaspoon of the filling in the centre of each circle.
Fold circle in half and press edges together. Place your finger against the fold and bring corners together, pressing to seal. Let stand for 10 minutes. In a large saucepan or pasta pot bring
3 qt/3 l water to boiling. Add half the tortellini. Reduce heat slightly. Boil, uncovered, for
6 to 8 minutes, or till al dente, stirring occasionally. Remove pasta from boiling water with
a slotted spoon and place in a greased casserole. Cover and keep warm in a preheated 300°F/
150°C oven while cooking remaining pasta.

■ Meanwhile, for sauce, in a small saucepan melt margarine or butter. Stir in flour. Add milk
all at once. Cook and stir till thickened and bubbly. Cook and stir for 1 minute more. Stir in
Swiss cheese and parsley till cheese is melted.

■ Spoon sauce over hot cooked tortellini and serve immediately.

Serves 4 as a main course

Per serving: 317 calories, 17 g protein, 24 g carbohydrate, 17 g total fat (6 g saturated), 115 mg cholesterol, 592 mg sodium,
316 mg potassium

STEPS AT A GLANCE	Page
MAKING PASTA	8–14
STUFFING PASTA	88

98

Agnolotti Florentine with Mornay Sauce

*A*gnolotti ("fat little lambs") and ravioli are essentially the same dish, except that the former are shaped into half-moons while ravioli are square. Tomato or spinach pasta (page 14) complements the spinach filling and the creamy cheese sauce.

■ For spinach agnolotti, prepare fresh pasta as directed, except roll each portion of the dough into an 8x12-in/20x30-cm rectangle. Cover and set aside. In a food processor bowl or blender container process or blend cooked spinach and 1 egg till nearly smooth. Transfer mixture to a medium mixing bowl and stir in cream cheese, prosciutto, Parmesan cheese, and nutmeg. Cover and refrigerate till needed.

■ Cut dough into circles with a 2-in/5-cm fluted cutter, place about ½ teaspoon of filling on each round, brush edge with water, then fold in half to create a half-moon shape. Repeat with remaining pasta and filling.

■ For Mornay sauce, in a small saucepan melt margarine or butter. Stir in flour. Add milk all at once. Cook and stir over medium heat till thickened and bubbly. Cook and stir for 1 minute more. Stir in fontina or Jarlsberg cheese till melted. Keep warm.

■ Meanwhile, in a large saucepan or pasta pot bring 3 qt/3 l water to boiling. Add half the pasta. Reduce heat slightly. Boil, uncovered, for 8 to 10 minutes, or till al dente, stirring occasionally. Remove pasta from boiling water with a slotted spoon and place in a greased casserole. Cover and keep warm in a preheated 300°F/150°C oven while cooking remaining pasta. Spoon Mornay sauce over hot cooked pasta and serve at once.

Serves 6 as an accompaniment or entrée

Per serving: 304 calories, 15 g protein, 18 g carbohydrate, 19 g total fat (7 g saturated), 140 mg cholesterol, 283 mg sodium, 199 mg potassium

Preparation Time: 1½ hours
Cooking Time: 16 to 20 minutes

INGREDIENTS

SPINACH AGNOLOTTI

4	PORTIONS (1 LB/500 G) TOMATO *OR* SPINACH PASTA (PAGE 14)
5	OZ/155 G FRESH SPINACH *OR* FROZEN CHOPPED SPINACH, COOKED AND WELL DRAINED
1	EGG YOLK
3	OZ/90 G PACKAGED CREAM CHEESE WITH CHIVES, SOFTENED
1	OZ/30 G FINELY CHOPPED PROSCIUTTO
2	TABLESPOONS GRATED PARMESAN CHEESE
1/8	TEASPOON GROUND NUTMEG

MORNAY SAUCE

2	TABLESPOONS MARGARINE *OR* BUTTER
2	TABLESPOONS PLAIN FLOUR
10	FL OZ/315 ML MILK
4	OZ/125 G SHREDDED FONTINA *OR* JARLSBERG CHEESE

99

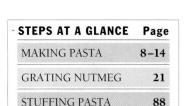

STEPS AT A GLANCE	Page
MAKING PASTA	8–14
GRATING NUTMEG	21
STUFFING PASTA	88

Rounds of pasta dough are stamped out with a scalloped cutter, filled with spinach, ham, and cheeses, then folded into charming half-moons.

Cheese Tortellini with Sausage & Peppers

Preparation Time: 45 minutes
Cooking Time: 20 minutes

INGREDIENTS

12	OZ/375 G ITALIAN-STYLE SAUSAGES
8	FL OZ/250 ML WATER
4	OZ/125 G CHOPPED ONION
2	CLOVES GARLIC, MINCED
2	TEASPOONS OLIVE OIL *OR* COOK-ING OIL
28	OZ/875 G TINNED ITALIAN-STYLE TOMATOES, CUT UP, WITH JUICE
2	FL OZ/60 ML TOMATO PASTE
2	FL OZ/60 ML DRY RED WINE
2	TABLESPOONS CHOPPED FRESH PARSLEY
1	TEASPOON DRIED OREGANO, CRUSHED
1/4	TEASPOON CRUSHED RED PEPPER (CHILI) FLAKES
1	MEDIUM GREEN PEPPER (CAPSICUM), CUT INTO 1/2-IN/12-MM PIECES
12	OZ/375 G DRIED *OR* 16 OZ/500 G FRESH CHEESE-FILLED TORTEL-LINI *OR* RAVIOLI, *OR* SPINACH AGNOLOTTI (PAGE 99)

*T*his deep-red spicy sauce isn't shy. It is assertively seasoned with crushed red pepper, garlic, and wine, a nice contrast to the mildness of the cheese-filled tortellini.

■ In a large frying pan combine sausages and water. Bring to boiling; reduce heat. Cover and simmer for 15 minutes, or till juices run clear. Drain off water. Cook sausages, uncovered, for 2 to 4 minutes more, or till brown, turning frequently. Remove from pan; cool. Bias-slice into ½-in/12-mm pieces. Wipe pan clean with paper towels.

■ In the same pan, cook onion and garlic in hot oil till tender but not brown. Stir in tomatoes, tomato paste, wine, parsley, oregano, and crushed red pepper flakes. Add sausage and green pepper to pan. Bring to boiling; reduce heat. Cover and simmer for 20 minutes, or to desired consistency.

■ Meanwhile, in a large saucepan or pasta pot bring 3 qt/3 l water to boiling. Add pasta. Reduce heat slightly. Boil, uncovered, 15 minutes for dried pasta or 8 to 10 minutes for fresh, or till al dente, stirring occasionally. (Or, cook according to package directions.) Drain immediately. Return pasta to warm saucepan. Pour sausage mixture over hot cooked pasta. Serve immediately.

Serves 4 to 5 as a main course

Per serving: 654 calories, 35 g protein, 73 g carbohydrate, 24 g total fat (6 g saturated), 111 mg cholesterol, 1,441 mg sodium, 946 mg potassium

100

Sausage and peppers, a very compatible duo, stand out in a highly seasoned tomato sauce for cheese tortellini.

Ravioli with Walnut Sauce

Grated fresh ginger, quickly sautéed with chopped onion and walnuts, adds a refreshing note to an easy pasta dish. Top with tangy crumbled blue cheese or feta cheese.

STEPS AT A GLANCE	Page
MAKING PASTA	8–14
STUFFING PASTA	88
CRUMBLING CHEESE	39

Preparation Time: 15 minutes
Cooking Time: 3 to 4 minutes

INGREDIENTS

9	OZ/280 G PURCHASED FRESH RAVIOLI *OR* HOMEMADE MUSHROOM-FILLED RAVIOLI (PAGE 96) *OR* MEAT- STUFFED RAVIOLI (PAGE 97)
1	OZ/30 G CHOPPED WALNUTS, PECANS, *OR* ALMONDS
4	SPRING ONIONS, THINLY SLICED
1	TEASPOON GRATED GINGER ROOT
3	TABLESPOONS MARGARINE *OR* BUTTER
1-1/2	OZ/45 G CRUMBLED BLUE CHEESE, FETA CHEESE, *OR* GRATED PARMESAN CHEESE (OPTIONAL)

101

*U*sing *bought fresh ravioli makes this a quick and easy meal to whip up after a busy day. If you prefer, serve the sauce over your own homemade ravioli (pages 96 and 97).*

■ In a large saucepan or pasta pot bring 3 qt/3 l water to boiling. Add pasta. Reduce heat slightly. Boil, uncovered, for 6 to 8 minutes, or till al dente, stirring occasionally. (Or, cook according to package directions.) Drain immediately.

■ Meanwhile, in a medium frying pan cook and stir the nuts, onions, and ginger in hot margarine or butter for 3 to 4 minutes, or till onions are tender but not brown and nuts are lightly toasted. Pour nut mixture over hot cooked ravioli. If desired, sprinkle with blue cheese, feta cheese, or Parmesan cheese. Serve immediately.

Serves 4 as a main course

Per serving: 360 calories, 13 g protein, 21 g carbohydrate, 25 g total fat (4 g saturated), 59 mg cholesterol, 538 mg sodium, 79 mg potassium

Manicotti with Roasted Vegetables

To make fresh manicotti shells, use two portions (about 8 oz/250 g) of Homemade Pasta (page 14). Roll dough into a 14x10-in/35x25-cm rectangle about ⅛ in/3 mm thick. Cut the dough into eight 5x3½-in/13x9-cm rectangles. Cook for 2 to 3 minutes and continue as directed, following the directions for filling manicotti on page 91, step 4.

■ Cut the peppers into bite-size strips. Cut the onion into small wedges. Bias-slice the squash and zucchini or courgettes into ¼-in/6-mm-thick pieces. In a 13x9x2-in/33x23x5-cm baking dish combine the peppers, onion, squash and zucchini or courgettes, and garlic. Drizzle with olive oil or cooking oil. Bake in a preheated 425°F/220°C oven for about 30 minutes, or till tender, stirring once or twice. Remove garlic cloves. Reduce oven temperature to 350°F/180°C.

■ Meanwhile, if using classic tomato sauce, prepare as directed. Set aside. In a large saucepan or pasta pot bring 3 qt/3 l water to boiling. Add manicotti shells. Reduce heat slightly. Boil, uncovered, about 18 minutes, or till al dente, stirring occasionally. (Or, cook according to package directions.) Drain immediately. Rinse with cold water and drain again.

■ In a medium mixing bowl stir together the eggs, mozzarella cheese, ricotta cheese, Parmesan cheese, chives, and pepper. To fill manicotti shells, spoon equal portions of the cheese mixture into each one. Arrange manicotti in a 3-qt/3-l rectangular baking dish. Pour tomato sauce over the top. Arrange roasted vegetables on top of the sauce. Bake, covered, in the 350°F/180°C oven for 35 to 40 minutes, or till heated through.

Serves 4 to 6 as a main course

Per serving: 720 calories, 41 g protein, 67 g carbohydrate, 34 g total fat (14 g saturated), 174 mg cholesterol, 885 mg sodium, 1,726 mg potassium

102

Preparation Time: 1 hour (includes sauce)
Baking Time: 65 to 75 minutes

INGREDIENTS

1/2	A MEDIUM GREEN PEPPER (CAPSICUM)
1/2	A MEDIUM ORANGE OR RED PEPPER (CAPSICUM)
1/2	A MEDIUM YELLOW PEPPER (CAPSICUM)
1/2	A MEDIUM ONION
1	MEDIUM YELLOW SQUASH AND
1	MEDIUM ZUCCHINI, OR 2 COURGETTES
2	CLOVES GARLIC, PEELED
1	TABLESPOON OLIVE OIL OR COOKING OIL
	CLASSIC TOMATO SAUCE (PAGE 18) OR 28 FL OZ/875 ML TINNED OR BOTTLED ITALIAN-STYLE TOMATO SAUCE
8	DRIED MANICOTTI SHELLS
2	BEATEN EGGS
8	OZ/250 G SHREDDED MOZZARELLA CHEESE
12	OZ/375 G RICOTTA CHEESE
1-1/2	OZ/45 G GRATED PARMESAN CHEESE
2	TABLESPOONS CHOPPED FRESH CHIVES
1/4	TEASPOON GROUND WHITE OR BLACK PEPPER

Green peppers, squash and zucchini (courgettes), and tomatoes add the bright colours and sun-drenched flavours of an Italian kitchen garden to cheese-filled manicotti.

Grilled Spinach Cannelloni

Preparation Time: 1 hour
Grilling Time: 5 minutes

INGREDIENTS

CANNELLONI

1	PORTION (4 OZ/125 G) HOMEMADE PASTA (PAGE 14)
5	OZ/155 G FRESH SPINACH *OR* FROZEN CHOPPED SPINACH, THAWED
3	OR 4 CLOVES GARLIC, PEELED AND QUARTERED
2	TABLESPOONS OLIVE OIL *OR* COOKING OIL
1	OZ/30 G GRATED PARMESAN CHEESE
2	TABLESPOONS FINE DRY BREAD CRUMBS
1/8	TEASPOON GROUND RED PEPPER (CAYENNE)
2	TEASPOONS OLIVE OIL *OR* COOKING OIL
1	TABLESPOON GRATED PARMESAN CHEESE

SAUCE

4	FL OZ/125 ML CHICKEN STOCK
1-1/2	TEASPOONS CORNFLOUR
1	TEASPOON MARGARINE *OR* BUTTER
1	TABLESPOON LEMON JUICE
1	TABLESPOON HEAVY (DOUBLE) CREAM
1-1/2	OZ/45 G TOASTED PINE NUTS

*T*o save time, use 6 dried lasagne noodles instead of making the fresh pasta. Cook the noodles according to package directions and drain. Cut each noodle into 3 pieces for 9 servings. Spoon the filling onto the pasta and continue as directed in the recipe.

■ For cannelloni, prepare and roll homemade pasta as directed. Cut into sixteen 3-in/7.5-cm squares. Cover and set aside.

■ Trim and wash fresh spinach (if using); finely chop. In a large frying pan cook and stir garlic in 2 tablespoons hot olive oil or cooking oil over medium-high heat for 30 seconds. Add fresh or thawed frozen spinach. Cook and stir for 1 to 2 minutes, or till fresh spinach is wilted or thawed spinach is heated through. Drain thoroughly in a colander, squeezing out excess liquid. In a medium mixing bowl combine spinach, 1 oz/30 g Parmesan cheese, bread crumbs, and ground red pepper.

■ Meanwhile, in a large saucepan or pasta pot bring 3 qt/3 l water to boiling. Add pasta. Reduce heat slightly. Boil, uncovered, for 3 to 4 minutes, or till al dente, stirring occasionally. Use a slotted spoon to carefully lift pasta out of water and into a colander. Rinse with cold water. Drain well. Carefully spread on a damp cloth towel.

■ To assemble, place 1 scant tablespoon filling along one end of each pasta square. Roll the dough tightly around the filling. Place on a greased baking sheet. Drizzle 2 teaspoons olive oil or cooking oil over pasta. Sprinkle with 1 tablespoon Parmesan cheese. Grill 6 in/15 cm from the heat for 5 minutes, or till golden brown.

■ Meanwhile, for sauce, in a small saucepan combine chicken stock and cornflour; add margarine or butter. Cook and stir till thickened and bubbly. Stir in lemon juice and cream and heat through. Spoon over cannelloni; sprinkle with toasted pine nuts.

Serves 8 as an accompaniment or entrée

Per serving: 182 calories, 7 g protein, 20 g carbohydrate, 10 g total fat (2 g saturated), 10 mg cholesterol, 147 mg sodium, 261 mg potassium

103

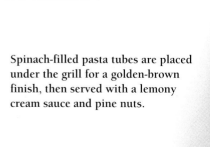

Spinach-filled pasta tubes are placed under the grill for a golden-brown finish, then served with a lemony cream sauce and pine nuts.

Classic Cannelloni

Both the tomato sauce and chicken filling can be prepared a day ahead and refrigerated until you assemble the cannelloni. Let the sauce and filling sit at room temperature for about 15 minutes so they will bake in the specified time.

■ Prepare and roll homemade pasta as directed. Cut into sixteen 3-in/7.5-cm squares. Cover and set aside.

■ Prepare classic tomato sauce as directed. Set aside. For Parmesan sauce, in a small saucepan melt margarine or butter. Stir in flour, salt, and pepper. Add milk all at once. Cook and stir over medium heat till thickened and bubbly. Stir in Parmesan cheese and sour cream. Set aside.

■ For chicken filling, heat oil in a large frying pan. Add chicken, onion, parsley, garlic, salt, and pepper. Cook for 5 minutes, or till chicken is tender and no longer pink and onion is tender. Cool slightly. Place chicken mixture and prosciutto or ham in a food processor bowl or blender container. Process or blend till mixture is finely chopped. Transfer filling to a medium mixing bowl and stir in 6 fl oz/185 ml of the Parmesan sauce.

■ In a large saucepan or pasta pot bring 3 qt/3 l water to boiling. Add pasta. Reduce heat slightly. Boil, uncovered, for 3 to 4 minutes, or till al dente, stirring occasionally. Drain.

■ Place a scant 2 tablespoons of the chicken filling along one edge of each pasta square. Roll dough tightly around the filling. Place in a greased 3-qt/3-l rectangular baking dish. Pour remaining Parmesan sauce over half the pasta. Pour tomato sauce over remaining pasta. Sprinkle with 1 tablespoon Parmesan cheese. Bake in a preheated 350°F/180°C oven for 30 to 35 minutes, or till heated through. Serve immediately.

Serves 4 as a main course or 8 as an accompaniment or entrée

Per serving: 490 calories, 27 g protein, 35 g carbohydrate,
28 g total fat (10 g saturated), 81 mg cholesterol,
1,066 mg sodium, 964 mg potassium

Two sauces, one made with fresh
tomatoes and the other a béchamel,
top homemade cannelloni.

STEPS AT A GLANCE	Page
MAKING PASTA	8–14
PREPARING SAUCE INGREDIENTS	16
MAKING TOMATO SAUCE	18
STUFFING MANICOTTI & CANNELLONI	90

Preparation Time: 1½ hours
Baking Time: 30 to 35 minutes

INGREDIENTS

1	PORTION (4 OZ/125 G) HOMEMADE PASTA (PAGE 14)
12	FL OZ/375 ML CLASSIC TOMATO SAUCE (PAGE 18) *OR* TINNED *OR* BOTTLED ITALIAN-STYLE TOMATO SAUCE

PARMESAN SAUCE

2	OZ/60 G MARGARINE *OR* BUTTER
1	OZ/30 G PLAIN FLOUR
1/4	TEASPOON SALT
1/8	TEASPOON PEPPER
12	FL OZ/375 ML MILK
1-1/2	OZ/45 G GRATED PARMESAN CHEESE
3	TABLESPOONS SOUR CREAM

CHICKEN FILLING

1	TABLESPOON OLIVE OIL *OR* COOKING OIL
8	OZ/250 G BONELESS, SKINLESS CHICKEN BREAST HALVES (FILLETS), CHOPPED
2	OZ/60 G CHOPPED ONION
1	OZ/30 G CHOPPED FRESH PARSLEY
1	CLOVE GARLIC, MINCED
1/4	TEASPOON SALT
1/8	TEASPOON PEPPER
2	OZ/60 G SLICED PROSCIUTTO *OR* HAM, CHOPPED
1	TABLESPOON GRATED PARMESAN CHEESE

104

Pasta Salads

Steps in Making Pasta Salads

COLANDER

SERVING BOWL

SCREW-TOP JAR

SERVING FORK
AND SPOON

BASIC TOOLS FOR MAKING PASTA SALADS

Always drain pasta thoroughly in a colander
or strainer before tossing with other ingredients in a wide, shallow bowl. A small glass
jar with a lid is handy for blending and storing salad dressings.

Not surprisingly, pasta has the same affinity with
salad dressings as it does with other sauces. Bathed
in herb-flavoured emulsions of fruity olive oil and tart
vinegar, or tossed with creamy yogurt or sour cream
blends, pasta absorbs some of the dressing and releases
wonderful flavour with each bite. The tender chewi-
ness of pasta contributes substance and textural contrast to a salad and holds its own against other additions
like ripe olives, crunchy bits of celery and pepper, chunks
of spicy salami, and toasted chopped nuts.

Pasta salads are delicious warm-weather companions
to grilled meats, poultry, and fish. As main courses, they
make appealing light lunches or suppers when accom-
panied with sliced fruit and a good, crusty loaf. They
are simple to put together and can be assembled just far
enough in advance to marry the flavours.

Pasta for salad should always be cooked just until al
dente, never a second more. Nothing is worse than
pasta that is too soft or that falls apart when the salad
is tossed together. Drain the pasta thoroughly as soon
as it is done, then rinse to stop the cooking and prevent
the pasta from sticking together. Give it a good shake
in the colander to pull off any water that remains. If
water clings to the pasta, the flavour of the dressing will
be diluted, much as it is when mixed with salad greens
that haven't been dried properly.

If the dressing calls for olive oil, use a good one. The
best are extra-virgin oils, from the first pressing of the
olive. These oils vary in their fruitiness and offer a spec-
trum of colour that ranges from verdant green to a
golden bronze. Purchase small amounts of several different kinds until you find one or two that please you.
Experiment with vinegars as well. A wide variety are
available to give your dressings excitement, from deep-
toned, sweet and mellow balsamic to red and white wine
vinegars with delicate infusions of herbs or fruit.

drain away as much water as possible after rinsing so none remains to dilute the dressing

dressings with a mayonnaise base blend better when whisked in a bowl

STEP 1 RINSING PASTA

Cook the pasta in 3 qt/3 l of rapidly boiling water until it is al dente. Immediately drain off the cooking water. Rinse under cold running water to separate the pasta; drain again thoroughly.

STEP 2 MAKING SALAD DRESSING

Place all ingredients in a glass jar with a lid. Secure the lid and shake vigorously until the ingredients are combined into an emulsion.

107

mix thoroughly, but with a light touch

STEP 3 TOSSING SALAD

Place all the salad ingredients in a wide, shallow serving bowl. Pour the dressing over the pasta mixture. With a large spoon and fork or two spoons, toss gently to coat all the ingredients with dressing.

Although this salad (page 116) specifies crinkled radiatori ("radiators"), you can substitute conchiglie ("shells") or any pasta of the same approximate size.

Curried Orzo Salad

Preparation Time: 25 minutes
Cooking Time: 5 to 8 minutes
Chilling Time: 2 to 24 hours

INGREDIENTS

6	OZ/185 G ORZO PASTA
5	OZ/155 G CHOPPED PROSCIUTTO OR COOKED HAM
2	ORANGES, PEELED, SECTIONED, AND CUT INTO BITE-SIZE PIECES
5	OZ/155 G CHOPPED CELERY
2	OZ/60 G CHOPPED GREEN PEPPER (CAPSICUM)
4	SPRING ONIONS, THINLY SLICED
2-1/2	OZ/75 G MAYONNAISE OR SALAD DRESSING
2-1/2	OZ/75 G PLAIN YOGURT
2	TABLESPOONS CHUTNEY, CHOPPED
3/4	TEASPOON CURRY POWDER
1	TO 2 TABLESPOONS MILK (OPTIONAL)
2	OZ/60 G PEANUTS

Here we've used orzo, a barley-shaped pasta, in place of rice for a colourful and refreshing salad with an Indian flavour. Other tiny pasta, such as rosamarina or riso, can also be used.

■ In a large saucepan or pasta pot bring 3 qt/3 l water to boiling. Add pasta. Reduce heat slightly. Boil, uncovered, for 5 to 8 minutes, or till al dente, stirring occasionally. (Or, cook according to package directions.) Drain immediately. Rinse with cold water; drain again thoroughly.

■ In a large bowl combine cooked pasta, prosciutto or ham, oranges, celery, pepper, and spring onions.

■ In a small mixing bowl stir together mayonnaise or salad dressing, yogurt, chutney, and curry powder. Stir into pasta mixture. Cover and refrigerate for 2 to 24 hours.

■ Just before serving, if necessary, stir in milk to moisten salad. Sprinkle with peanuts before serving.

Serves 6 as an accompaniment or entrée

Per serving: 328 calories, 11 g protein, 33 g carbohydrate, 18 g total fat (2 g saturated), 8 mg cholesterol, 384 mg sodium, 236 mg potassium

STEPS AT A GLANCE	Page
COOKING PASTA	12
SECTIONING AN ORANGE	108
MAKING PASTA SALADS	106

108

STEPS IN SECTIONING AN ORANGE

STEP 1 CUTTING THE PEEL FROM AN ORANGE

Slice off the top and bottom of an orange with a sharp paring knife. Set one flat end on a cutting board. Hold the orange and, working from top to bottom, cut off 1-in/2.5-cm-wide strips of peel.

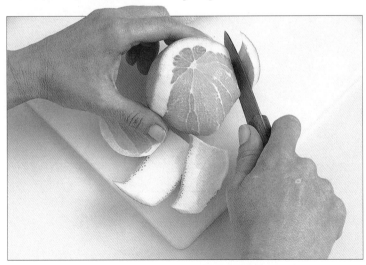

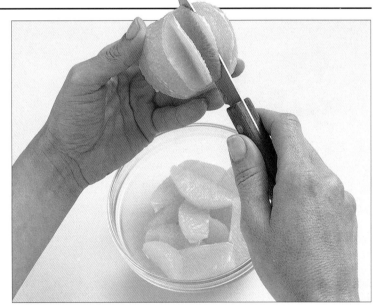

STEP 2 SECTIONING AN ORANGE

Work over a bowl to catch the juice. Insert a paring knife between the flesh and membrane of one section. Cut down to the centre of the fruit. Turn the knife and slide it up the other side of the section to release it from the membrane on that side. Repeat with remaining sections.

Serve any grilled chicken or fish with this pasta salad that features the flavours of an Indian curry.

Big pasta shells filled with fresh vegetables are easily eaten in the fingers.
They are ideal buffet fare.

110

Eggplant Salad Shells

Preparation Time: 1¼ hours
Chilling Time: 2 to 24 hours
Cooking Time: 23 to 25 minutes

STEPS AT A GLANCE	Page
PREPARING SAUCE INGREDIENTS	16
TOASTING NUTS	39
COOKING PASTA	12
STUFFING SHELLS	111

*M*ake this earthy eggplant (aubergine) filling the night before so that all the flavours have a chance to mix. Serve as an hors d'oeuvre, or as part of a cold buffet.

■ In a large frying pan cook eggplant (aubergine), onion, and celery in hot oil, covered, over medium heat for 5 to 8 minutes, or just till tender, stirring occasionally. Stir in the undrained tomatoes, wine vinegar, tomato paste, sugar, salt, and red pepper. Cook, uncovered, over low heat for 5 minutes, or to desired consistency, stirring occasionally. Remove from heat. Stir in parsley and capers. Cool. Cover and refrigerate for 2 to 24 hours.

■ Let the eggplant (aubergine) mixture stand at room temperature for 30 minutes. Stir in olives and pine nuts.

■ Meanwhile, in a large saucepan or pasta pot bring 3 qt/3 l water to boiling. Add pasta shells. Reduce heat slightly. Boil, uncovered, for 23 to 25 minutes, or till al dente, stirring occasionally. (Or, cook according to package directions.) Immediately drain. Rinse with cold water; drain again thoroughly. Pat dry with paper towels.

■ To assemble, fill each shell with equal amounts of the eggplant (aubergine) mixture. Serve immediately.

Makes 18 shells

Per serving: 235 calories, 5 g protein, 28 g carbohydrate, 13 g total fat (2 g saturated), 0 mg cholesterol, 381 mg sodium, 472 mg potassium

INGREDIENTS

1	MEDIUM EGGPLANT (AUBERGINE), PEELED AND CUT INTO 1/2-IN/12-MM CUBES
1-1/2	OZ/45 G CHOPPED ONION
1-1/2	OZ/45 G CHOPPED CELERY
2	FL OZ/60 ML OLIVE OIL *OR* COOKING OIL
14	OZ/440 G TINNED DICED PEELED TOMATOES, WITH JUICE
3	TABLESPOONS RED WINE VINEGAR
2	TABLESPOONS TOMATO PASTE
1	TEASPOON SUGAR
1/2	TEASPOON SALT
	DASH GROUND RED PEPPER (CAYENNE)
1	TABLESPOON CHOPPED FRESH PARSLEY
1	TABLESPOON CAPERS, DRAINED
2-1/2	OZ/75 G SLICED PITTED BLACK *OR* KALAMATA OLIVES, PITTED AND SLICED
2	TABLESPOONS TOASTED PINE NUTS *OR* CHOPPED ALMONDS
18	CONCHIGLIONI (LARGE PASTA SHELLS), ABOUT 4 OZ/125 G

111

STEP IN STUFFING SHELLS

STEP 1 STUFFING SHELLS

Cup a cooked pasta shell in one hand and squeeze at both ends to open it. Scoop up some of the filling with a small spoon and insert into the shell. Repeat with the remaining shells and filling.

Hero Pasta Salad

Preparation Time: 20 minutes
Cooking Time: 8 to 12 minutes

INGREDIENTS

SALAD

3	OZ/90 G ROTINI, CAVATELLI, *OR* OTHER DRIED SHAPED PASTA
4	OZ/125 G CUBED PROVOLONE CHEESE
2	OZ/60 G COOKED HAM, CUT INTO THIN BITE-SIZE STRIPS
2	OZ/60 G HARD SALAMI, CHOPPED
1	SMALL RED ONION, HALVED THEN SLICED
4	OZ/125 G PEPPERONCINI, SLICED, *OR* SLICED BELL PEPPER (CAPSICUM) RINGS
6	OZ/185 G SHREDDED ICEBERG *OR* ROMAINE (COS) LETTUCE
1	LARGE TOMATO, COARSELY CHOPPED, *OR* 4 OZ/125 G CHERRY TOMATOES, HALVED

DRESSING

3	TABLESPOONS OLIVE OIL *OR* SALAD OIL
3	TABLESPOONS BALSAMIC VINEGAR
1	TABLESPOON CHOPPED FRESH OREGANO *OR* 1/2 TEASPOON DRIED OREGANO, CRUSHED
2	SMALL CLOVES GARLIC, MINCED
1/4	TEASPOON DRY MUSTARD
1/8	TEASPOON COARSELY GROUND BLACK PEPPER

*T*his salad lends itself well to improvisation. Try adding some sliced kalamata olives, capers, chopped peppers, or yellow or orange tomatoes. If making it ahead, wait to add the lettuce and tomato until just before serving time.

■ In a large saucepan or pasta pot bring 3 qt/3 l water to boiling. Add pasta. Reduce heat slightly. Boil, uncovered, for 8 to 12 minutes, or till pasta is al dente, stirring occasionally. (Or, cook according to package directions.) Drain immediately. Rinse with cold water and drain again thoroughly.

■ In a large bowl toss together cooked pasta, provolone cheese, ham, salami, onion, and pepperoncini or pepper rings. Add lettuce and tomato; gently toss to mix.

■ In a screw-top jar combine olive oil or salad oil, vinegar, oregano, garlic, dry mustard, and pepper. Cover; shake well. Pour over pasta mixture; toss to coat all ingredients with dressing and serve.

Serves 4 as a main course

Per serving: 426 calories, 20 g protein, 30 g carbohydrate, 25 g total fat (9 g saturated), 39 mg cholesterol, 1,080 mg sodium, 449 mg potassium

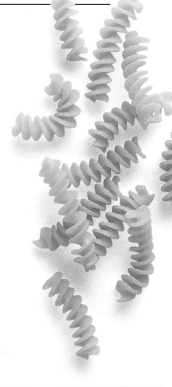

STEPS IN SHREDDING LETTUCE AND SLICING ONION

STEP 1 SHREDDING LETTUCE

Hold one quarter of a head of iceberg lettuce firmly against a cutting board. Using a sharp knife, slice the lettuce thinly. The slices will separate into long, thin shreds.

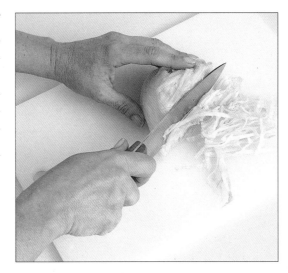

STEP 2 SLICING ONION

Peel the onion and cut in half lengthwise from top to root end. Place on a cutting board, cut-side down. Hold firmly and cut crosswise into ⅛-in/3-mm-thick slices. The slices will separate into half circles and then in pieces.

A mixed salad is always more interesting
when the shapes, colours, and textures vary.
Here rotini attractively contrast with other
ingredients cut into cubes, thin strips,
and half-rounds.

Grilled Tuna & White Bean Salad

This is no ordinary tuna salad. It combines fresh tuna with cannellini beans, tomatoes, yellow pepper, and penne pasta, all bathed in a lemon-and-herb dressing.

Preparation Time: 30 minutes
Grilling Time: 4 to 6 minutes
Cooking Time: 12 to 14 minutes

INGREDIENTS

12	OZ/375 G FRESH *OR* FROZEN TUNA STEAKS, 1/2 IN/12 MM THICK, *OR* 12 OZ/375 G TINNED WHITE TUNA, DRAINED AND BROKEN INTO CHUNKS
	OLIVE OIL *OR* SALAD OIL
8	OZ/250 G PENNE *OR* OTHER DRIED SHAPED PASTA
4	FL OZ/125 ML OLIVE OIL *OR* SALAD OIL
2	FL OZ/60 ML LEMON JUICE
20	OZ/625 G TINNED CANNELLINI *OR* WHITE KIDNEY BEANS, DRAINED AND RINSED
2	MEDIUM TOMATOES, COARSELY CHOPPED
1/2	A MEDIUM YELLOW PEPPER (CAPSICUM), CUT INTO THIN BITE-SIZE STRIPS
2	SHALLOTS, FINELY CHOPPED
2	TABLESPOONS CHOPPED FRESH BASIL *OR* 1 TEASPOON DRIED BASIL, CRUSHED
1/4	TEASPOON SALT
1/8	TEASPOON PEPPER

*I*f you have any leftover salad, refrigerate it, but be sure to bring it back to room temperature before serving it again, or the dressing will be thick and lumpy.

■ If using tuna steaks, thaw if frozen. Measure thickness of fish. Brush each side of tuna with oil. Grill tuna for 4 to 6 minutes per ½-in/12-mm thickness, or till tuna flakes easily when tested with a fork, turning once. Slice tuna diagonally into thin strips.

■ In a large saucepan or pasta pot bring 3 qt/3 l water to boiling. Add pasta. Reduce heat slightly. Boil, uncovered, for 12 to 14 minutes, or till al dente, stirring occasionally. (Or, cook according to package directions.) Drain immediately.

■ In a large bowl combine cooked fresh or tinned tuna, hot cooked pasta, beans, tomatoes, and sweet pepper.

■ For dressing, in a screw-top jar combine 4 fl oz/125 ml olive oil or salad oil, lemon juice, shallots, basil, salt, and pepper. Pour dressing over pasta; toss gently and serve.

Serves 4 to 6 as a main course

Per serving: 519 calories, 16 g protein, 59 g carbohydrate, 28 g total fat (4 g saturated), 1 mg cholesterol, 369 mg sodium, 493 mg potassium

STEPS AT A GLANCE	Page
COOKING PASTA	12
MAKING PASTA SALADS	106

114

Warm Tomato–Feta Cheese Salad

Preparation Time: 50 minutes
Cooking Time: 10 to 12 minutes

INGREDIENTS

3	RIPE TOMATOES *OR* 6 RIPE PLUM (ROMA) TOMATOES, SEEDED AND CHOPPED
3	TABLESPOONS OLIVE OIL *OR* SALAD OIL
3	TABLESPOONS LEMON JUICE
1/2	OZ/15 G CHOPPED FRESH OREGANO *OR* 1 TEASPOON DRIED OREGANO, CRUSHED
2	CLOVES GARLIC, MINCED
1/8	TEASPOON PEPPER
2	OZ/60 G KALAMATA OLIVES, PITTED AND CHOPPED, *OR* PITTED BLACK OLIVES, CHOPPED
8	OZ/250 G CRUMBLED FETA CHEESE
8	OZ/250 G DRIED FARFALLE *OR* CONCHIGLIE, *OR* 16 OZ/500 G FRESH FARFALLE

*P*asta goes Greek. For a stronger and more authentic Greek flavour, use kalamata olives rather than pitted black olives. If you refrigerate any leftover
salad, bring it to room temperature before serving.

■ Drain chopped tomatoes in a strainer for 15 minutes to remove excess liquid.
In a large mixing bowl whisk the olive oil or salad oil into the lemon juice. Stir in
oregano, garlic, and pepper. Add drained tomatoes, olives, and feta cheese. Toss to
mix. Let mixture stand at room temperature for 30 minutes.

■ Meanwhile, in a large saucepan or pasta pot bring 3 qt/3 l water to boiling. Add
pasta. Reduce heat slightly. Boil, uncovered, for 10 to 12 minutes for dried pasta
or 2 to 3 minutes for fresh, or till al dente, stirring occasionally. (Or, cook according
to package directions.) Drain immediately. Return pasta to warm saucepan. Add
tomato mixture to hot cooked pasta and toss to mix. Serve immediately.

Serves 8 to 10 as an accompaniment or entrée

Per serving: 346 calories, 14 g protein, 29 g carbohydrate, 20 g total fat (10 g saturated), 57 mg cholesterol, 741 mg
sodium, 187 mg potassium

115

Warm pasta tossed with marinated
tomatoes, olives, and cheese makes
a salad that's full of flavour.

Pasta Salad with Walnut Dressing

Preparation Time: 30 minutes
Cooking Time: 10 to 12 minutes

INGREDIENTS

8	OZ/250 G TRICOLOURED OR PLAIN RADIATORI
4	OZ/125 G CHOPPED TOASTED WALNUTS
4	OZ/125 G CAPICOLLO OR COOKED HAM, CUT INTO SMALL CUBES
4	OZ/125 G CRUMBLED BASIL-AND-TOMATO FETA CHEESE OR PLAIN FETA CHEESE
2-1/2	OZ/75 G PITTED RIPE OLIVES OR UNSTUFFED GREEN OLIVES
2	FL OZ/60 ML OLIVE OIL OR SALAD OIL
2	FL OZ/60 ML FRESH LIME JUICE
1/2	OZ/15 G CHOPPED FRESH PARSLEY
1	CLOVE GARLIC, MINCED
1/4	TEASPOON SALT
1/8	TEASPOON PEPPER
	RED-TIPPED (OAK) LEAF LETTUCE

*V*olunteer to bring this easy salad when you're asked to a casual gathering. Combine the ingredients at home, but don't add the dressing until you get to the party.

■ In a large saucepan or pasta pot bring 3 qt/3 l water to boiling. Add pasta. Reduce heat slightly. Boil, uncovered, for 10 to 12 minutes, or till al dente, stirring occasionally. (Or, cook according to package directions.) Drain immediately. Rinse with cold water; drain again thoroughly.

■ In a large bowl combine pasta, walnuts, capicollo or ham, feta cheese, and olives.

■ In a screw-top jar combine oil, lime juice, parsley, garlic, salt, and pepper. Cover and shake well. Pour over pasta mixture and gently toss to coat all ingredients with dressing. Serve salad on lettuce leaves.

Serves 4 as a main course

Per serving: 691 calories, 24 g protein, 55 g carbohydrate, 44 g total fat (9 g saturated), 42 mg cholesterol, 922 mg sodium, 425 mg potassium

STEPS AT A GLANCE	Page
COOKING PASTA	12
CRUMBLING CHEESE & TOASTING NUTS	39
MAKING PASTA SALADS	106

116

A dressing tangy with lime coats chunks of ham and cheese, olives, toasted walnuts, and multi-coloured pasta.

Tortellini-Mozzarella Salad

Little leaves of radicchio serve as edible bowls for individual portions of tortellini salad.

Preparation Time: 20 minutes
Cooking Time: 15 minutes

INGREDIENTS

5	OZ/155 G DRIED *OR* 10 OZ/315 G FRESH MEAT-FILLED TORTELLINI
6	OZ/185 G CUBED PLAIN *OR* SMOKED MOZZARELLA
1/2	A MEDIUM RED *OR* YELLOW PEPPER (CAPSICUM), CUBED
1/2	OZ/15 G CHOPPED FRESH BASIL *OR* 1 TEASPOON DRIED BASIL, CRUSHED
3	TABLESPOONS OLIVE OIL *OR* SALAD OIL
2	TABLESPOONS WHITE WINE VINEGAR
1	TABLESPOON BALSAMIC VINEGAR
1	SMALL HEAD RADICCHIO, DIVIDED INTO LEAF CUPS, *OR* 4 LARGE LETTUCE LEAVES

117

*I*f you need to make the salad ahead of time, reserve the mozzarella and add it right before serving time so it doesn't become mushy or rubbery.

■ In a large saucepan or pasta pot bring 3 qt/3 l water to boiling. Add pasta. Reduce heat slightly. Boil, uncovered, 15 minutes for dried pasta and 8 to 10 minutes for fresh, or till al dente, stirring occasionally. (Or, cook according to package directions.) Drain immediately. Rinse with cold water; drain again thoroughly.

■ In a medium mixing bowl combine cooked tortellini, mozzarella cheese, and red or yellow pepper.

■ In a screw-top jar combine basil, oil, white wine vinegar, and balsamic vinegar. Cover; shake well. Pour over pasta mixture and gently toss to coat all ingredients with dressing. Serve salad in radicchio cups or on lettuce leaves.

Serves 4 as a main course

Per serving: 320 calories, 15 g protein, 21 g carbohydrate, 19 g total fat (8 g saturated), 46 mg cholesterol, 381 mg sodium, 206 mg potassium

STEPS AT A GLANCE	Page
COOKING PASTA	12
MAKING PASTA SALADS	106

GLOSSARY

The following glossary provides information on selecting, purchasing, and storing ingredients used in this book. Groups of ingredients are arranged clockwise from the upper left and are described in the text accordingly.

ARTICHOKES Only the fleshy base of the leaves and the meaty bottom of this edible bud of a tall, thistle-like plant are eaten; the rest of the leaf and the fuzzy interior choke are discarded. Artichokes are sold fresh in sizes ranging from very small to very large; they are also available frozen, tinned, and marinated. Select compact, heavy globes with tightly closed leaves; refrigerate in a plastic bag for up to 4 days.

ASPARAGUS This tender stalk with a tightly closed bud is prized for its delicate flavour and subtle hue (white asparagus, a delicacy, is not as common). Crisp, straight, firm stalks with a tight cap are best. Wrap in damp paper towels and refrigerate in a plastic bag for up to 4 days.

BASIL With its affinity for sauces and tomato-based dishes, it isn't surprising to find basil in many pasta recipes. Intensely aromatic, fresh basil arrives in summer, when tomatoes are at their peak; dried basil may be found on the spice shelf all year. Store freshly cut stems in a little water, cover with plastic, and refrigerate for up to 2 days.

BROCCOLI Both the rigid green stalks and the tightly packed dark green or purplish-green heads (also called florets) are edible. Choose firm stalks and closed heads with deep colour and no yellow areas. Refrigerate in a plastic bag for up to 4 days.

CANNELLINI BEANS Also known as white kidney beans, these are mild-flavoured and meaty when cooked, and available dried or tinned.

CAPERS The pickled flower buds of a Mediterranean bush, capers add a piquant note to foods. Most markets stock them in jars with other condiments. Store opened jars in the refrigerator. Before using, drain off their vinegar brine.

CARROTS Choose firm, bright orange carrots; avoid those that are limp or have cracks or dry spots. Refrigerate in a plastic bag, tops removed, for up to 2 weeks. Peel or scrub before using. Tiny baby carrots are actually a separate variety prized for their delicate flavour and charming appearance. Store them as you would large carrots.

CHEESES The following cheeses often appear in pasta dishes. *Mascarpone* is rich and buttery, a cross between cream cheese and sour cream. Pliable, stringy *mozzarella* is used in baked dishes and salads. *Parmesan* is a hard and crumbly grating cheese with a nutty flavour; it is used as the finishing touch on most pasta dishes. Moist *ricotta* is mild and semi-sweet, with a soft, creamy texture. *Romano* is similar to Parmesan, but is sharper in taste. Storage length varies with the type of cheese, but all cheeses must be wrapped well and refrigerated to stay fresh.

CHIVES The long, hollow green leaves of this herb add bright colour and a mild onion flavour to many dishes when chopped into pieces. Fresh chives should not be wilted or damaged. Refrigerate, wrapped in damp paper towels and then in a plastic bag, for 3 to 4 days.

FENNEL With its tubular stalks and feathery leaves, this bulbous, creamy-white to pale-green vegetable resembles celery, but its flavour hints of licorice. Fresh fennel is delicious raw or cooked, while dried fennel seed is used as a seasoning. Select bulbs that are free of cracks or brown spots. Refrigerate in a plastic bag for up to 4 days.

ARTICHOKES

ASPARAGUS

BASIL

BROCCOLI

CANNELLINI BEANS

CAPERS

CARROTS

CHEESES

CHIVES

FENNEL

118

GARLIC A bulb with a papery outer skin, a head of garlic is composed of numerous small cloves. Garlic may be used as a savoury seasoning for almost every course of a meal. It is aromatic and almost bitter when raw, but becomes delicate and sweet when cooked. Fresh garlic should be plump and firm. Store whole bulbs in a cool, dark, dry place.

GINGER ROOT The rhizome, or underground stem, of a semitropical plant, fresh ginger root is a pungent seasoning with a lively, hot flavour and peppery aroma. Select stems that are firm and heavy, never shrivelled, with taut, glossy skin. Wrap in a paper towel and refrigerate for up to 2 days. For longer storage, wrap airtight and freeze the unpeeled root.

KALE A member of the cabbage family, kale has ruffled dark green leaves and tastes like its cabbage relatives. It is eaten fresh or cooked, or used as a decorative garnish. Wash the leaves in cold water, dry, then refrigerate in a paper towel–lined plastic bag for up to 3 days.

OLIVE OIL A staple of Mediterranean cooking, olive oil imparts a clean, fruity flavour and golden-to-green colour to salad dressings, grilled bread, and pasta sauces. Use extra-virgin oils, from the first pressing, for cold dishes. For sauces, use milder oils that can stand up to heat. Store in a dark spot away from heat for 6 months, or in the refrigerator for a year. (Chilled oil may get thick and cloudy; let it warm to room temperature before using.)

OREGANO Packed with robust flavour and aroma, oregano is a favourite herb of Italian and Greek cooks. Select bright green fresh oregano with firm stems. Look for dried whole or ground oregano with other spices. Refrigerate fresh oregano in a plastic bag for up to 3 days.

PANCETTA Unlike regular bacon, mild, spicy-sweet Italian pancetta is rarely smoked, although it is usually seasoned with pepper. It is sold in delicatessens in a roll rather than in a flat slab. Refrigerate it, well wrapped, for several weeks.

PARSLEY Widely used for cooking and garnish, parsley has such a clean, refreshing flavour that it is sometimes enjoyed as an after-meal digestive. Curly-leaf parsley is mild, while Italian parsley is flat-leafed and more pungent. Select healthy, lively looking bunches. To store, rinse and shake dry, wrap in paper towels and a plastic bag, and refrigerate for up to 1 week.

PROSCIUTTO This spicy, air-dried Italian ham is either eaten raw in paper-thin slices or heated as part of a recipe. Top-quality *prosciutto di Parma* is imported from Italy, but excellent domestic varieties are also available. Any Italian delicatessen and some gourmet food shops will stock both types. Wrap and refrigerate it for several weeks.

SQUASH/COURGETTES Soft-skinned, slender green and yellow zucchini (courgettes), straight and crookneck squashes, and pattypan squashes are classified as "summer" vegetables, although many are sold year round. They can be used interchangeably. Choose heavy, well-shaped squash without cracks or bruises. Refrigerate for up to 4 days.

TOMATOES Botanically a fruit, tomatoes are eaten as a vegetable. Oval-shaped plum tomatoes (also called Italian or Roma) are thick and meaty, with less juice and smaller seeds than other varieties, which makes them ideal for sauces. They are sold fresh, or in tins sometimes flavoured with basil and other seasonings. Other tinned or bottled forms include tomatoes cooked with celery, onions, and seasonings; tomato paste, a highly concentrated purée; and sweet, chewy dried tomatoes, either plain or oil-packed.

GARLIC

GINGER ROOT

KALE

OLIVE OIL

OREGANO

PANCETTA

PARSLEY

PROSCIUTTO

SQUASH/COURGETTES

TOMATOES

119

INDEX

Recipes

Steps

120

USING THE NUTRITION ANALYSIS

Keep track of your daily nutrition needs by using the information we provide at the end of each recipe. We've analysed the nutritional content of each recipe serving for you. When a recipe gives an ingredient substitution, we used the first choice in the analysis. If it makes a range of servings (such as 4 to 6), we used the smaller number. Ingredients listed as optional weren't included in the calculations. To convert calories to kilojoules, multiply by a factor of 4.2.